TELFORD

PICTURES FROM THE PAST

TELFORD

PICTURES FROM THE PAST

BY TOBY NEAL AND PHIL GILLAM

irst published in Great Britain byThe Breedon Books Publishing Company Limited
Breedon House, 44 Friar Gate, Derby, DE1 1DA. 1999

This paperback edition published in Great Britain in 2015 by DB Publishing, an imprint of
JMD Media Ltd

ISBN 978-1-78091-500-5

Printed and bound in the UK by Copytech (UK) Ltd Peterborough

CONTENTS

Most of the pictures in this book have come from the files of Shropshire Newspapers. However, we are grateful to the following people who also contributed: Ray Farlow, Ray Pritchard, Elaine Bradshaw, Peter Dickinson, Norman Kelsey, Jean Beard, Vic Hordley, Ken Oakley, and Alan Harper.

INTRODUCTION

TELFORD: Pictures From The Past may seem a strange title, almost a contradiction in terms. How can a new town, a town which has developed within the span of a generation, have any past worth speaking of? Yet look beyond the ever-expanding Telford shopping centre, the mirrored glass office blocks, and the hangar-like factories, and investigate further than the blanket of new housing, and you will find that Telford has another heartbeat. The truth is that Telford is not a new town built from scratch in a virgin landscape. It is a number of proud old Shropshire towns which have been melded into one unit by glueing them together with new bits.

Older residents remember the days before their lives were turned upside down and their traditional communities were changed forever. Often they are bitter that the familiar and much-loved has been replaced by the garish and new in the name of progress.

Then there are the incomers, who know nothing of Telford's past, and judge it – favourably or unfavourably – for what it is now, rather than what it used to be. Happily the newspaper photographers of the day got busy with their cameras when it became apparent in the early 1960s that east Shropshire was going to be transformed. Their images, many of which are reproduced here, will be fascinating for young and old alike, giving an insight into how things used to be, and charting the changes which have created the town today. Most of the photographs have come from the archives of Shropshire Newspapers. Indeed, the *Shropshire Star*, which was launched in October 1964, has grown up more of less hand in hand with the new town, which was designated in 1963.

Telford has now come of age. Thousands of planted saplings have become trees, roadside bulbs give a profusion of colour in spring and – and here's the real test – there is even talk of knocking down some buildings in the town centre because they are 'out of date'. The first chapters have been written. But the Telford story continues.

Toby Neal
July 2002

THE WAY WE WERE

BACK in the 18th century, east Shropshire was the cradle of the industrial revolution, and a huddle of towns grew up and expanded amid a landscape which was scarred and exploited. These were working towns, and as industries declined, the relics of the area's industrial heritage were left like souvenirs of an earlier age. There was an explosion of council house building amid the old pit mounds and spoil heaps in the immediate post-war period. For instance, Wellington Urban Council's 1,000th house at 18 Mount Gilbert was opened in 1952. This was for many families the first time they had had an indoor bathroom and toilet. Yet mains electricity and mains water were by no means universal and slum conditions were prevalent. Two towns in particular had so much in common that they could almost be regarded as sister towns. Madeley and Dawley lie only a couple of miles apart. Both were working class communities, with High Streets packed with shops, and an employment backbone of foundries, industry and mining. And, although Dawley folk had their own dialect in the 'Dawley twang' (e.g. 'Ow thee bist, jockey? for How are you my friend?), they more or less spoke the same language. How these towns would have evolved naturally over the years, we shall never know. Because they were about to be hit by an earthquake.

Edith Pargeter at work behind the counter in Bemrose's chemists shop in Dawley in 1936. Her first book, *Hortensius, Friend of Nero,* had just been published. Miss Pargeter had been born in Wellington Road, Horsehay, and was destined to become one of the most popular British novelists of the 20th century with her *Brother Cadfael* series of books written under the pseudonym Ellis Peters. Her brother Ellis Pargeter was chairman of Dawley Urban District Council in the late 1940s. They both resigned from the Labour Party in 1949 because they felt the party had deserted its Socialist principles. Edith lived most of her adult life in Madeley and died in 1995. Notice the fascinating array of products on the shelves, ranging from Zints Digestive Mints, to Meritor, Shavex, and a hot water bottle.

Donnington Village in 1938. The metal plate in the road was a public weighbridge which was run by a George Hayward, and there was a coal wharf to the right of where the photographer is standing. In fact the area of the picture was known as Coal Wharf. The cyclist is probably coming from May (or Maisie) Shepherd's paper shop. Behind the photographer was a railway line which came from The Grange and Granville pits bringing the coal, and there was a level crossing on the road. The building on the right was a Primitive Methodist Church which is these days used as a Serbian Orthodox Church. On the left in the distance is the Midland Iron Works, C&W Walker Ltd, which has been demolished and replaced with housing within the last few years.

In February 1939 it was officially announced that a £1 million 'war depot' was to be built at Donnington. A huge Army stores complex called Central Ordnance Depot, Donnington, was created – and meant a major building scheme was needed to give the workers homes. The newly created housing area was known as 'New Donnington', a name which stuck for some time after the war, although the entire area is now known simply as Donnington. The Army base is still there, employing thousands of civilians. This picture taken at Donnington – the location was censored in wartime – must date from around 1942 or 1943 when Minister of Health Ernest Brown performed the opening ceremony of a 'self-contained community of 844 new houses for war workers transferred from London for a new industry in the Midlands.' Each house had an eighth of an acre of garden, electric light and power, running water, and mains drainage, at a maximum weekly rent of 17s 9d. 'There is already a fine shopping centre, complete with Post Office,' the original caption continued.

Oakengates in the 1950s, looking up under the railway bridge towards Bridge Street and Hartshill. The area in the foreground has disappeared under a new ring road. The building on the right with the clock was at one time the post office. At the time of this picture the sign in the corner window appears to read 'Oakengates Conservatives Rooms'. The buildings on the right were demolished as part of the town's redevelopment.

Let's travel back to 1928 to meet the little girls of Hadley County Primary School. Unusually, this picture has been captioned right to left, beginning in the top right hand corner, across each row in turn, and finishing in the bottom left hand corner. We begin then with the lady who is presumably the teacher, Miss Arnold. And then the little angels are: Jean Barker, Marie Stokes, Doris Houlston, Mareel Purcell, Marie Wakeley, Elsie Beard. Middle row, from right: Nellie ?, Vera ?, Daisy Stringer, Kathleen Potter, Gladys Gregory, Ivy Bedow, Gwen Shirley, Joyce Abel, Mabel Horris. Bottom row: Madge Parsons, Doris Smitherman, Mary Stringer, Doris Ball, Irene Greatholder, Nellie Overton, Joan Tidman, and Betty Elliott.

The old Red Church at Jackfield in May 1939. Built in 1759 on a knoll overlooking the Ironbridge Gorge and dubbed the 'red' church because of its red brick construction, it became unsafe because of mining underneath which caused cracks to open up in the structure. By 1900 it was rarely used, if at all, and remained derelict, with cows sheltering inside, until it was demolished in the early 1960s. The church was said to be haunted and in October 1949 brothers Doug and Max Jones, who lived nearby, decided to have a bit of fun when they heard some folk were going to stage a 'ghostwatch'. They lightened one of their mother's old dresses with whitening and attached string or wire to the tower so that their home-made apparition would descend in a convincingly spooky way at midnight. Unfortunately they were rumbled before their little scheme reached its haunting climax.

Madeley Court in July 1959 and the owner Mr Joseph Barnett is quoted as saying: 'I am attached to the old house.'

'Wellington's new council offices' at Tan Bank. They were opened on April 24, 1940, by Wrekin MP Colonel James Baldwin-Webb. This photograph must date from around then – notice the wartime blackout cover on the car headlight in the foreground. The new offices meant that for the first time since being formed in 1894, the council had its own home. By this time it had an administrative patch, including Ketley and Donnington areas, of 89 square miles, with a population of 16,955. The urban part of Wellington was covered by Wellington Urban District Council. East Shropshire Water Board was also to meet at the Tan Bank offices, which are now occupied by social services. Wellington UDC and Wellington RDC disappeared under local government reorganisation which saw the creation of Wrekin Council in 1974. Colonel Baldwin-Webb, who was deputising at the opening for the Minister of Health, was drowned in September 1940 when the liner he was on as a passenger was torpedoed in the Atlantic.

This strange landscape is photographed from Ketley Bank, looking towards Oakengates in August 1958. Here, grass grows slowly over the mounds left by the industry of years long gone. Everywhere can be seen derelict chimneys and workings gradually crumbling as nature reclaims her own.

The King's Barn, affectionately known as Charlie's Loft – adjoins the Coventry Gauge and Tool Company's works at Madeley. Charles II slept in the barn during his flight after defeat at the Battle of Worcester in 1651. 'It is now used,' says the original caption from November 1958, 'as a canteen for the work people. The picture shows canteen staff tidying-up after lunch yesterday.' Coventry Gauge and Tool has long since departed and the site has been redeveloped as flats.

A photograph from 1954 of the quaint booking office at Admaston railway station which was cleverly built into the arch of the bridge.

Heavy traffic struggles through the narrow streets of Admaston village in the October of 1965. Villagers were campaigning at the time for a bypass, but never got one.

Pat Farran fills a glass with the salty water from the remaining spring at the Admaston spa. The year is 1963.

A chimney-top view of Wellington taken from the cab of a tall crane working in Queen Street and showing the Wrekin behind the rooftops. It's December 1962.

The Free Bridge at Jackfield, seen here in March 1954, was built in 1909. It was Shropshire's first reinforced concrete bridge. It was called the Free Bridge because there was no toll. By the 1980s the structure had seriously deteriorated. The increase in traffic had also made it out of date, because it was too narrow for two-way traffic – drivers would have to wait for the first motorist on the bridge to cross. Very occasionally two stubborn motorists would meet in the middle and there would be an entertaining stand-off. As a temporary solution to the structural problems, a metal Bailey bridge was laid on the top of the deck, and traffic lights were installed. A permanent solution came on October 18, 1994, when a modern Jackfield Bridge, built alongside the site of the old structure, was opened. The Free Bridge was demolished, but a small section was saved and stands for posterity on the south bank, close to the site of a little shack of a shop which was for generations a familiar feature on the approach to the old bridge.

Park Avenue, Madeley, in 1943. The Anstice Memorial Hall is behind the trees on the left. The row of shops on the right was demolished to make way for the new Madeley District Centre. This road used to be the main street through the town.

A view of Coalbrookdale looking towards Paradise and Dale End in September 1959. Part of Coalbrookdale Works dominates the picture, with the railway line beyond.

A nice view from June 1938 of the Coalport China Works alongside the River Severn. By this time the works had been abandoned, production having ended in 1926. They now form part of the Ironbridge Gorge Museum.

Alderman T.H. Thompson, the Mayor of the Borough of Wenlock, reads the Proclamation at The Square, Ironbridge, on the accession of Edward VIII to the throne. It was to prove to be a very short reign. This photograph was first published in the *Wellington Journal and Shrewsbury News* on January 25, 1936. Behind Ald. Thompson is Ironbridge war memorial. At some stage the war memorial was moved from this position over to the other side of the road, to a site on the approaches to the Iron Bridge, where it remains to this day.

According to the original caption, this picture from March 5, 1958, shows the Bush Lane estate, at Dawley, which 'has been described as reflecting little credit on the council or the tenants. The estate is said to be in a deplorable condition with the hundreds of tin sheds and rubbish.' It is the present day Langley Crescent, and today new homes are crammed in to the area in the foreground. Note the ever-present spoil mounds in the background.

New housing going up in May 1959 on the Langley Farm estate at Dawley. Dawley had been earmarked in 1956 as a potential site for 3,000 new homes to take 'overspill' from Birmingham. The first two of these Birmingham 'overspill' families moved to new homes on this estate on November 15, 1958. And Dawley Urban District Council's 1,000th council house was handed over at 4 Oxford Road in 1959. This view shows Lancaster Avenue under construction. And Dawley New Town – the forerunner of Telford – was still years away!

Another view of developing Dawley, but this time we are about half a mile away from the previous view, and are looking at the Manor Farm estate in January 1956. Pit mounds were levelled to make space for council housing. This scene is looking towards Windsor Road.

A Pilot Motors bus pulls away from the new bus station in Oakengates in September 1954. In the background is the remnants of a huge slagheap called the Charlton Mound which was cleared during the 1930s. The slope of the much-reduced mound that was left was planted with shrubs in 1938, but as it is barren in this shot 16 years later, perhaps they didn't grow. In the distance on the extreme left further spoil mounds can be seen, underlining how much derelict land there used to be in this district.

Bert Ryder of Broseley standing on the sunken wreck of a rock-filled lighter – small boat – as he fishes on the River Severn at Jackfield in September 1959. The river water was exceptionally low at the time, revealing the outline of the barge. It may have been sunk deliberately. Jack Owen of Broseley recalls working in the Maws fitting shop in about 1932 and wandering down to see the remains of two lighters in his dinner hour after foreman Jack Morgan told him how they had been filled with rocks and rubble and sunk near the Boat Inn years beforehand to bolster the riverbank.

A very bare-looking Wellington Market Hall, probably soon after World War Two.

A march past by the Home Guard in Park Street, Madeley, during wartime – notice that one of their number is out of uniform! It is being led by Mr B. Scoltock, who was the first headmaster of Madeley Modern School. On the right of the parade is Mr Fred Key, who used to live in Victoria Road, and on the left is a Mr Owen, from Park Lane. They are passing the West End Cinema, which was originally known as the Parkhurst Cinema. One of those taking the salute, on the right of the group in front of the cinema, may be a Captain Nutt, who was one of the management at the Court Works in Madeley.

A look up Madeley High Street in about 1938 – posters on the left are for two films from that year, John Boles in *Sinners in Paradise* and Will Hay in *Hey! Hey! USA*. Station Road is to the left. This photograph was taken by Flo Jones, whose parents ran the newsagents in Exchange House, which is the building on the corner on the left. Her father Jack was killed in a road accident in March 1936. Before becoming a newsagents it was the Royal Exchange pub, run by Albert and Oretta Harrington, but the pub closed around 1930. The pub had another storey, but this was removed around the time of its closure or not long after, probably because it was unsafe. Next to the pub with a large window is the old club room which was used for dances. In the 1960s and 1970s Exchange House was home to Harrod's newsagents but these days it is a tandoori restaurant.

For years this junction at the centre of St Georges was considered an accident blackspot. The crossroads are seen here in July 1962, with C.E. Rigby's drapers store on the corner of West Street to the left, and on the right, which is Church Street, the Oakengates and District Co-operative Society stands on the corner. At the site of Rigby's there was previously a bakers run by a man called Mr Christmas who delivered by horse and cart, which led to the inevitable joke locally along the lines that 'Christmas is coming'. On the corner of Church Street there used to be a butchers run by a Mr Molineux. In earlier times, there was, believe it or not, a lamp-post standing more or less in the middle of the road at this junction in what was known then as St Georges Square. Despite campaigns and petitions throughout the 1960s and later, traffic lights were not installed and the traffic hazards were eventually solved by demolishing Rigby's and part of the Co-op building opposite to improve visibility, and putting in a mini roundabout.

Incidentally, St Georges is a new name for the village, which was previously called Pain's Lane. The decision to change the name to St George's – the dropping of the apostrophe is a fairly recent practice – was taken at a meeting at the George Inn on December 19, 1859. One of the reasons put forward for the change was that 'a man could not bring the lass he loved to a Pain's Lane.'

Mr Sam Bradley, 76, and his wife Edith, in the garden of their crumbling home at Jackfield in April 1964. The heart of the village was suffering a slow but sure death due to a landslip towards the River Severn.

Flashback to December 10, 1952, the year in which the Jackfield landslip really began to take hold. It was first noticed by a train driver at the start of the year who saw that the railway tracks through the village were becoming distorted. By April 1952 it was clear a crisis was at hand when Pear Tree Cottage split asunder. It was the first to go. Some villagers in the worst affected part of Jackfield – the area known as The Square – tried to carry on life as normal but in the end a number of residents had to move out because their homes were unsafe, and a number of properties had to be demolished. It is estimated that at least 16 homes were lost, including the local post office, which is on the left of this shot. The land movement problem in Jackfield is still a live issue which continues to worry residents today.

Photographs of old railway stations always seem to be especially evocative. Perhaps it's because so many of us have spent so much of our time on platforms, perhaps trainspotting as youngsters, welcoming people home, saying fond farewells to loved ones, or just waiting for trains for what would become memorable journeys. This then is Trench Crossing railway station pictured on an undated postcard.

Disappeared Ketley. This is the view westwards along Station Road – the old A5 – in the late 1940s or early 1950s. We are standing by what were known for years as the Seven Stars traffic lights. Just left of centre in the distance is the Wesleyan Chapel, which was also known as the Central Methodist Church. All the buildings on the right hand side of the road visible here have disappeared. They were replaced in the 1960s by a church, and flats, including the high-rise Reynolds House development, all set much further back from the road. Out of picture left of the road sign was a fish and chip shop, which was quite recently replaced by a modern successor. And although we cannot see them, other shops on the left hand side of the road were the Co-op, a junk shop, a bike shop kept by cycling champion Ernie Clements, which later became Jack Parton's barbers, and Alf Whittingham's grocery shop. The railway crossed the road in the distance and in the station house lived Bill Pearson and his family. His wife gave piano lessons to local children

Another undated postcard and a shot of Woodhouse Pits, Oakengates.

King Street in Dawley showing The Royal Cinema. Built in 1937, it was one of the few in the area which was purpose-built. The first film shown is thought to have been Keep Your Seats Please starring George Formby. The other cinema in Dawley was The Cosy, irreverently known by some as the Flea Pit. This was the old camp cinema from the Prees Heath army camp near Whitchurch which was dismantled and re-erected at Dawley, where it opened in Burton Street in 1921 as the town's first 'proper' cinema. The owners were Mr A. Pendleton and Mr J.C. Williams. The Cosy appears to have kept going into the 1950s and was still standing in 1956, but was probably demolished soon after. The site is now a car park. The Royal has gone the way of so many old-style cinemas, and is a bingo hall.

Mr and Mrs F. Jarvis of 11 High Street, Ironbridge, and (far right) their little dog, pictured outside their shop. Date unknown.

Waterloo Street in Ironbridge, perhaps around the 1920s or 1930s, looking up towards St Luke's Church. The building on the right is the Crown Inn. It was doomed in March 1973 when Woodside licensing committee refused to renew its licence on structural grounds. It was then demolished, together with the adjoining buildings, and the site is now a car park. The large building a little further along on the same side of the street was taken down and totally rebuilt in the same style around a new inner shell about three years ago.

A peaceful rural scene looking towards The Wrekin in 1947 or 1948 across fields which were destined not long after this to become covered with housing. A youthful Peter Dickinson, who was born and bred in Wellington, took this picture with his Kodak 116 Autographic camera from a spot partly down a lane which is now North Road, and looking over a stud farm which is now Parklands estate. Mr Dickinson rather wishes now that he had taken more pictures back in those far-off days before the open fields he knew so well in his youth around Wellington, Dothill, and Admaston, were built on.

Finger Road in Dawley, around the 1930s. Today it is full of road humps to slow the traffic. This part of Dawley is known as The Finger, a name it takes from a long-disappeared pub called 'Peter's Finger'. This pub name is a religious reference.

Walker Street in Wellington around 1902, which was the time of the opening of Wellington Library, which is on the left with the clutch of children standing outside. It was built to commemorate the coronation of Edward VII. Wellington's most famous librarian was the poet Philip Larkin, who was there from 1943 to 1946, and would often pop in to the Raven pub and joined the YMCA so he could use the snooker table. He had a serious girlfriend, 16-year-old Ruth Bowman, who was at Wellington High School and lived in Herbert Avenue. Larkin's comments about Wellington tended to be caustic, as was his way. 'I spend most of my time handing out tripey novels to morons,' he told a friend. Wellington has clearly forgiven him, and in January 1999 named an alley alongside the library in his honour.

Coalport ferry, which was replaced in 1922 by a war memorial footbridge linking Jackfield and Coalport. At one time there were many ferries taking passengers over the River Severn in Shropshire, but over time new bridges gradually killed them off, and floods were another hazard. In 1799 the Coalport ferry sank and 28 people drowned in what was the greatest single loss of life on the river.

BEFORE THE STORM

IT all seems to have begun in 1955, when an article appeared in a Birmingham newspaper raising the idea of Dawley becoming an 'overspill' area for the city. The idea had legs and before long Dawley was earmarked as a potential location for 3,000 houses to accommodate families from Birmingham. The first two 'overspill' families moved to Dawley on November 15, 1958, to new homes at the so-called Langley Farm Estate, which contains the present day roads of Lancaster Avenue and Gloucester Avenue. A concept began to grow in the minds of officialdom.

Dawley was, to their way of thinking, run down and declining further. So why not revitalise the area by making Dawley the hub of a new town, with a civic centre, new shops and, of course, new housing, created amid the vast swathes of derelict land?

These were the heady days of the 1960s, where sweeping away the old and bringing in the new was almost a mission and a crusade. The creation of Dawley New Town was announced in 1962. It was officially designated in 1963 and staff of Dawley Development Corporation, the government-appointed body set up to plan and build the town – bypassing all the usual planning channels and with a fat wallet of taxpayers' money – set up offices initially at Hartfield House, Doseley, and then after a year or so, at Priorslee Hall. Lines on the map showed that Dawley New Town would basically embrace the Madeley, Dawley and Ironbridge areas – a total of 9,100 acres – and was intended to take 50,000 people from the overcrowded West Midlands conurbation, giving a total population of about 90,000. To the north, Wellington and Oakengates were not included. And then… nothing. For a couple of years little happened. This was the calm before the storm.

A row of cottages in Dark Lane in January 1965. Dark Lane Methodist Chapel is in the background and was the hub of the whole community. This terrace was known as the 'Bottom Row'. All these homes were obliterated during the development of Telford town centre. This site lies under what it today the shopping centre and its car parks.

Another view of the lost community of Dark Lane, this time from a few years earlier. It is seen on September 7, 1962.

East meets West at Hadley Modern School in the spring of 1962. Thirteen-year-old Elaine Cadwallader strives to help find the answer for her 13-year-old friend, Gali Singh, from New Delhi, India, who was now living at Watling Street, Wellington. Gali had been living in England for the previous four years.

Mr R. Davies, the occupant of the only cottage still inhabited near the old kiln in Horsehay, holding one of the earthenware jars which used to be made there. The photograph was taken on September 6, 1962. The old kiln is more often known as the Horsehay Round House and it, together with a group of adjoining homes, were known locally as Horsehay Potteries. The original 1962 caption to this photograph said 'the kiln will shortly be demolished to make way for a new factory.' It was certainly demolished – some time around 1970, it seems – but not to make way for a factory.

Much of this was relatively new when the picture was taken in October 1960. These Dawley council houses had been built during the 1950s. In the foreground is Dawley Secondary Modern School, which opened in October 1956. The first headmaster was Mr Jim Rennie. It became Phoenix School, a comprehensive, in 1965. The Georgian-style building in the near distance, left, is Pool Hill School, which burnt down during the evening of July 31, 1977 and was never rebuilt. Phoenix was also hit by a major fire which destroyed the main hall, the canteen and gym – that's the entire block underneath the tall black chimney, working left off the picture – on December 29, 1995. In the far distance, centre, is the massive hangar-like building of Horsehay Works, known by various names in later years – Adamson Alliance, Adamson Butterley, and AB Cranes. Whatever you remember it as, it closed in early 1985 with the loss of 307 jobs and was demolished a couple of years later. The site is now used for housing and light industry. Notice the barren spoil mound in the foreground. Growth on these mounds in Dawley area is very slow, but these days they are covered with heather, scrub and some trees.

Many a visitor to Oakengates Theatre will recognise this bridge. The venue is just round the corner. But the story which led to the taking of this photograph back in 1962 was all about the railway bridge being 'a disgrace to the town' with some local councillors demanding it be tidied up. However, while some lambasted the bridge – built by the Lilleshall Company in 1848 – as 'unsightly and antiquated' there were other councillors who believed it should be scheduled as an ancient monument and cared for as such. In this case the conservation lobby won, as the bridge is still there and still catches out the occasional tall vehicle.

Rooms with a view. One reason why Dawley was considered an attractive location for new development was that the area was covered with old pit mounds, a legacy of the east Shropshire coalfield. This slagheap in or near Dawley was a particularly unwelcome neighbour for residents back in January 1965. In the event, many of the mounds have survived and been softened by nature, making them attractive landscape features.

Demolition in King Street, Dawley, in May 1959, looking towards the town centre. The area on the left is called The Hollow and all the buildings have been cleared away. A newly-built dental surgery stands there today. The buildings on the right have fared better, even down to the distinctive chimneys surviving. On the corner, over the road from the bus stop, is the Queens Head pub.

Closed, barred, and chained, the gates of Ketley Playing Fields are seen here in October 1964. The plan was to create Shropshire's finest athletics track on the barren site, with a projected opening date of 1967 and a cost of £50,000. It never happened. Wellington Rural District Council hatched the stadium scheme, but then when Telford Development Corporation was created, the council's dream did not fit in with the corporation's leisure plans for the new town, so a scaled-down version of the proposals was carried out including an outdoor swimming pool, golf driving range, pitch-and-putt, children's play area, football pitches, pavilion and meeting rooms, together with a scented rose garden for the blind. A note on the original print of this picture says 'gates now demolished, 1967'. Indeed the gates have disappeared, along with the stone pillars, but the Ketley Playing Fields sign survives at the entrance to a landscaped area, supported on metal lattice-work pillars.

The disappeared village of Hinkshay, probably in the late 1950s or early 1960s. On the right can be seen part of the Ever Ready factory, which opened in August 1956. The factory gatehouse is on the extreme right. The building which looks a bit like a school is in fact Hinkshay Mission Church and behind it is the factory canteen. The middle row of terraced homes was Single Row, the left hand row was Double Row, and the terrace in the distance, upper right, was New Row, nicknamed Ladies Row by locals. Everything in this view, including the factory, has been demolished and the site is now part of Telford Town Park.

The Local Public Inquiry into the proposed new town of Dawley was under way. This was November 1962 and here, objectors to the proposals, armed with their briefcases, maps and bundles of documents, were in the thick of it.

One of the blessings of the week for 78-year-old Miss Lucy Springall, of Wellington Road, Coalbrookdale – a good hot dinner brought by the meals-on-wheels service. The year was 1964.

A view over the river into Jackfield on December 5, 1963.

We are looking towards the site of what is today one of Telford's biggest housing estates. But this photograph was taken 40 years ago, when planners were drawing up their scheme for the new town. The farm and cow-filled fields on the horizon are now covered by the homes of the Brookside estate. In the dip is the Dawley to Bridgnorth road and the farm on the hill is Home Farm. The bridge on the far left carries a road which ran past Madeley Court and then over a railway line, the tracks of which can just about be made out between the buildings. The bridge today carries the Silkin Way footpath and cycle path, but all the buildings in this view have gone. The photograph was taken in 1962 or 1963.

Horsehay and Dawley Station on February 21, 1962, with Horsehay signal box nearest the camera.

The Captain Webb Memorial in Dawley has done some moving about over the years. It was unveiled in October 1909 to honour Dawley-born Captain Matthew Webb, the first man to swim the English Channel. In its original form it was a public drinking fountain with three glass hanging balls or lanterns, and its initial site was at the end of High Street outside the Lord Hill, quite close to Webb's birthplace, a house which has long been demolished. Here the memorial is pictured being re-erected in January 1958 a short distance away outside Dawley library. Watching in disgust is Frank Jones, Dawley born and bred, who was one of the many locals angered by the move, which was made to allow for road improvements at the New Street-High Street-King Street junction. Some time later the memorial was shifted yet again, this time to an out-of-the-way spot on Paddock Mount outside prefabricated council offices. When Dawley High Street was made traffic-free and revamped in 1980 the opportunity was taken to return the memorial to more or less its original position outside the Lord Hill.

Remember the bad winter of 1963? This photograph was taken during that big freeze, on January 17. Here is Dawley High Street, which was the main through route for traffic. Heavy lorries, buses, and vans came up Dun Cow Bank – off the shot to the left – and thundered through the narrow street. The pain was relieved in the summer of 1976 when Dawley bypass was opened.

The Cuckoo Oak road junction in Madeley on March 15, 1963. Notice the Halesfield pit mounds in the distance on the left, and the handsome large house – later to be destroyed by the creation of a roundabout, fire station and ambulance station – which stood at the corner of the turning to Shifnal.

Dawley Bank, with the Baptist Chapel on the left, on January 17, 1963. The Victorian chapel was demolished in March and early April 2000 and replaced with a new chapel and community centre roughly on the same site.

Well, this is certainly one way to cool down after an energetic jiving session! Twenty-three-year-old Dawley twins Mrs Valerie Collins and Miss Alwyn Jones at the Pyjamas Ltd party at the Majestic, Wellington, in December 1964.

We can do no better than quote directly from the reporter's eyewitness account which accompanied this picture of old Hollinswood in March 1965.

'Not 300 yards from the A5, you seem to lose a hundred years and take a sudden step backwards into the shadow of the industrial revolution. For the houses I was shown have no back doors, no bathrooms, and no running water.

'Water, when the tap is not frozen, must be drawn into buckets and carried from communal wash houses. Lavatories, shared in many cases, stand 20 paces away, down mossy paths. They are little more than holes in the ground, covered over by crumbling brick and tiled buildings.

'In a forgotten, man-made valley, from the days when iron and coal were torn from the earth, they lean among black and sinister slagheaps, like the pathetic remnants of a frontier shanty town. Together they make Regent Street (slums at the time in Wellington) look like Beverly Hills penthouses.'

And here is one of the families who lived in these homes. Mrs Sylvia Riordan stands at her front door with three of her four daughters.

Clearing the way for new business and industry at Ketley in August 1962. Quite frankly we've had trouble pinpointing the exactly location of this development, despite the various clues on the photo, such as the railway line in the distance and the works at the top left. Our failure to identify the spot might be a bit embarrassing – because this could well be the site of the *Shropshire Star* building. The *Shropshire Star* was launched in a purpose-built press and office complex at Ketley in October 1964, and our head office remains there still.

Holyhead Road, Oakengates, in March 1966. Where the photographer is standing is now a huge roundabout. But back in the 1960s this was a busy crossroads on the A5 and in 1973 a lorry smashed into the Greyhound pub on the left and became embedded. Nobody in the crowded bar was hurt and the driver jumped to safety, but the pub was so badly damaged that it had to be virtually rebuilt. After an 18 month closure, it reopened in June 1974. Its troubles were however not over. In 1991 rowdy behaviour and vandalism became so bad that a temporary manager and his family fled in fear and refused to return. The Greyhound closed around the mid-1990s and is today a takeaway pizza joint.

Market Street, Oakengates, on November 8, 1966. Check out some of the businesses – the Green Inn on the left, Orme & Sons, Woolworths, Dickins, and, on the right, George Mason's. Relatively speaking, these were good times for the town, whose traders were particularly badly affected by the creation of Telford Town Centre only a mile or so away, and the misguided introduction of an Oakengates ring road which turned the heart of the town into an island.

A pressing problem for Oakengates Urban Council in 1963 was the narrow and twisting bridge at Stafford Road which had no effective footpath and yet had to be used by children on their way to schools in the Wrockwardine Wood and Trench areas. The council had asked for something to be done to improve safety and – as a result – the county council had included in the year's estimates a sum for the provision of a new footbridge to run alongside the existing road bridge.

An unusual view of the busy Hadley crossroads taken from the top of a crane at work on a 12-storey block of flats in Hadley in 1966.

Operators in action at Oakengates Telephone Exchange in December 1964.

Looking down Lion Street, Oakengates, perhaps around 1960. The road to the left leads to the railway station, and to the right is Oxford Street, with the Co-op on the corner. The Co-op dominated Oakengates, occupying a number of different buildings throughout the town centre. In the upper floor of the building with a little tower in the distance at the bottom of the road was the dentist, Mr Fortune. On the lower floor was Ball's hardware store, and there was a shoe shop next door, and then next to that a greengrocer's. That building, together with the Brown Lion Inn on the left, were subsequently demolished.

It's March 1963 and foreign workers wishing to learn English are attending the first course to be held at the Walker Technical College, Oakengates. Here, the students, who all lived and worked in the Wellington area, are instructed by Mr G. Pickering.

Fields ripe for building on at Stirchley in October 1962. And built on they were. The housing estates of Stirchley and Randlay now cover the fields to the horizon. The Rose and Crown pub in the foreground now has a whole new clientele.

Looking from Dawley bus station at Paddock Mount across the spoil mounds towards Langley School, which is on the left. It later became Hinkshay School and, after considerable alterations, rebuilding, and general knocking about, was officially reopened under the name Mount Gilbert School in November 2001, catering for children with emotional and behavioural difficulties. The houses on the right were known as Bush Avenue, but have since changed their name.

A view from close to Beech Road, Madeley, looking across the fields which were soon to be transformed into the Woodside housing estate, the second and biggest of the housing estates of Telford New Town. The Wrekin is in the distance. The farm is clearly ready for the worst, as it is already in a state of some dereliction.

Dawley Urban Council's new bow-shaped block of flats in King Street, Dawley, being constructed in November 1964. Rumours that the flats were proving difficult to let were denied by the council. 'We will let them all eventually,' said a council spokesman.

Farmer Mr Eddie Bromley had washday blues back in 1964. 'It's whiter than white,' he said grimly as he gazed at a mammoth build-up of frothy, bubbly suds in the old lock of the Trench arm of the Shropshire Union Canal near his farm at Wappenshall. Mr Bromley, chairman of the Wellington branch of the National Farmers Union, was concerned about the suds, which built up to a height of 15 feet. When they appeared he contacted local NFU secretary Mr Sam Badger and a Severn River Board pollution officer. Said Mr Bromley: 'I'm worried in case it might have any effect on my livestock – and other people's.'

ADVENT

WORK on Dawley New Town officially began on November 15, 1965. The first place to be developed was the Tweedale industrial estate at Madeley. This was intended to be a beacon of modernity, demonstrating how 20th century workers could be employed in light and airy buildings rather than the dark and dirty sweatshops of the past. On March 8 the following year work began on building houses at Sutton Hill, which overlooks Madeley. Bulldozers and diggers tore up the ground exposing the red soil beneath. The north eastern part of the Sutton Hill estate was built first.

In the centre of the homes was schemed in a shopping precinct and community centre. The estate was enclosed within a vast circular perimeter road as the planners placed great store on keeping people and traffic as far apart as possible. Their dream was that nobody would have to cross a road with fast-moving traffic. Instead they could take an underpass.

Almost immediately the development was controversial. The homes were high-density and cheaply constructed, leading to claims that they would become the slums of the future. Strangely, Dawley Development Corporation was working piecemeal, without a master plan. It had a draft plan, the brainchild of consultant planner John Madin, and was working on a detailed plan when, in late 1965, the Government told it to stop. This was because a new report had recommended including Oakengates and Wellington in the new town, throwing the entire project up in the air. Rather than stop work on Tweedale and Sutton Hill, the corporation simply ploughed on and awaited developments. But the pace was tortoise-like. By May 1967, only 20 families were living on Sutton Hill and in the previous 12 months the population within the Dawley Urban District Council area had actually decreased by 120. And in November 1967 housing minister Anthony Greenwood said that Dawley New Town was making 'the least and slowest progress of any overspill area'. Oh dear. Dawley New Town was stagnating.

Dawley farmers pictured outside the Charlton Arms at Wellington in September 1962 where they gathered to discuss their response to the proposed takeover of their farmland so that 'Dawley New Town' could be built.

Although the new town is not officially under way (reads the original caption to this January 1962 photograph), Dawley Urban Council is already looking ahead to the days when its staff will be enlarged. It has bought this house opposite its present offices in King Street, Dawley, for extra office accommodation.

The Lord Hill at the end of Dawley High Street following the junction improvements which saw the removal of the Captain Webb Memorial. The black and white building on the left was soon to be demolished. This picture was taken in 1962 or 1963 – certainly before the *Shropshire Star* came along (in autumn 1964), because the newspaper billboard is for our sister paper, the Wolverhampton-based *Express & Star*.

Dawley Bank or Lawley Bank? It's a bit of a moot point to decide where one area ends and the other begins. Whatever you want to call it, this view dates from August 10, 1962.

Members of the Board of Dawley Development Corporation met for the first time in February 1963. Photographed at the private meeting in Birmingham Council House are (left to right, back row): Viscount Boyne of Burwarton; Sir Reginald Pearson, the chairman; Mr Christopher Cadbury, a member of the Midland New Towns Society; and Mr F.W. Kenchington, a Birmingham chartered surveyor; (left to right, front row): Mrs I. Martin Wilson, Salop County Council WVS organiser; and Alderman W.T. Bowen, chairman of the Birmingham Overspill Committee. The seventh member of the corporation board, missing from this picture, was Councillor Isaiah Jones, chairman of Wellington Rural District Council.

Not long now. An uncommon view of Madeley centre in the late 1960s, with the Anstice Memorial Hall on the right. Builders would soon move in to begin developing the park-like open space in the centre of this shot to create Madeley District Centre, which included supermarkets and a library.

An attractive rural scene looking towards Stirchley in October 1963. You can just make out the Norman St James' church at the heart of Stirchley Village, on the rising ground in the distance. Wrekin MP Bill Yates lived close by in the 18th-century Old Rectory. He emigrated to Australia in 1967. A strange urban myth has grown up that somehow he managed to take the old Wrekin Beacon with him and get it installed on Sydney Harbour Bridge. It's a nice tale, but sadly has not a grain of truth in it.

'Alone in Botany Bay spinney, Dawley, sits Mary Brown where, with her family, she often finds relaxation. Certainly more relaxation than was found by the early residents of the more famous 'Bay' in Australia. The Dawley spinney was once renowned for producing some of the best coal in Shropshire. But no-one seems to know how it got its name.' So says the original caption to this photo, which was taken in February 1962.

Dawley car park and bus station on August 15, 1962. Later the mound beyond the car was developed with demountable offices for Dawley Urban District Council.

Starting to plan. Mr John H.D. Madin, planning consultant of Dawley Development Corporation, and his assistant, Mr Lewis Jones, who is on the left, survey ruined industrial relics in December 1963. Within a decade these buildings at Blists Hill were protected for posterity by becoming part of the Ironbridge Gorge Museum.

They don't make dustbins like this any more. The rear of terraced cottages off the Dawley to Coalbrookdale road at Horsehay in February 1963.

Industrial dereliction near the site of the Wide Waters pool at Dawley in October 1962.

This is where the first bricks of Dawley New Town were to be laid. The picture was taken on or about April 2, 1965, at a location described as 'near Madeley'. It is then Sutton Hill, which was the first of the housing estates created on agricultural land overlooking Madeley. Work began on March 8, 1966, and the great gouges carved in the fields by the diggers revealed a red sandy soil underneath. In fact, strictly speaking, construction work on Dawley New Town had officially begun several months earlier, on November 15, 1965, at the Tweedale industrial estate. The gentleman on the right is a reporter from the *Shropshire Star* at the time, who was accompanying the photographer. It was not unusual for reporters to get roped in like this. You can imagine the conversation: 'I need somebody on my picture, go on, you'll do, I won't picture your face, look over there gazing into the distance…'

Sutton Hill estate taking shape on November 20, 1967.

Members of the Dawley New Town Society's study group meet for the first time in September 1964. They are seen here being addressed by Mr J.P. Bellingham at Madeley Modern School. They met to mull over ideas before the publication of the master plan for Dawley New Town.

Squadron Leader F.T. Cooper of RAF Shawbury hands over the keys of the Wrekin Beacon to Mr R.G. Lawson during a ceremony at the Wrekin summit in April 1965. Mr Lawson was a member of the Wrekin Beacon Preservation Trust executive committee. The famous beacon itself is in the background and had been turned off by the RAF at the stroke of the New Year as 1965 had dawned, but there was a public outcry and a committee was formed to revive it. The 'friendly light' was turned on again at Easter, but the money seems to have run out and the beacon was turned off forever. By 1970 the structure was derelict and was dismantled in August that year. A new beacon – in fact two lights on the revamped Wrekin telecommunications mast – was turned on at midnight to welcome in the new millennium at the start of the year 2000.

Bridge that gap. Work is under way on a new bridge at the bottom of Madeley High Street around May or June 1968. It was one of the early changes in Madeley brought about by the new town. The low railway bridge at the spot had been removed to be replaced with a modern arched structure to carry the Silkin Way footpath and cycleway (named after Lewis Silkin, who is credited as being the founder of Britain's New Towns) which used the old railway trackbed. Between the scaffolding can be seen the Prince of Wales pub, with its white frontage. The pub, together with all the other buildings visible through the scaffolding, was demolished to make way for a huge traffic island.

'A sad sight for some, but a relief for many more,' said the original caption to this photograph taken on February 2, 1968. It is unlikely that there are many Madeley residents today who consider the destruction of the old heart of the town a 'relief'. The picture captures the start of the demolition to make way for a new shopping centre in Madeley. 'It is the first redevelopment of an existing area in Dawley New Town,' the original caption went on. 'The properties affected are the Co-operative drapery store in Park Avenue, the old Post Office, the old people's rest room, numbers 1, 2, 3 and 4 Russell Road, and 11 and 12 Park Avenue.'

Fast forward over a year to the day when young visitors from St Mary's College, Bangor, came on a four-day visit to Telford new town, and looked around the emerging new Madeley centre on April 22, 1969.

There's still a glimpse of old Madeley centre's shops on the left – they must have been demolished very soon after this picture was taken – while the modern development grows up on the doorstep, in about April 1969.

The Queen unveils a plaque at the Sutton Hill housing estate in March 1967. Sir Reginald Pearson, chairman of the Dawley Development Corporation, is on the right of the picture.

A run-down and neglected stretch of road running alongside Oakengates railway station in 1968. The white building on the right of the picture is the Brown Lion inn.

Traffic on the A5 in Ketley in 1968. The fish and chip shop on the right of the picture is still trading today although the original premises seen here were replaced by a modern outlet just a couple of years ago. The road alignment has changed too. Nowadays the junction is a crossroads controlled by traffic lights with the Elephant and Castle pub (formerly the Seven Stars) dominating the scene. You can just see a pub sign on the left of the picture indicating the Seven Stars which is just out of shot. Just beyond the chip shop on the right (again out of shot) stands the *Shropshire Star's* head offices.

The work going on here was resurfacing of the road in Dawley High Street. The closure of the road – in April 1967 – sparked a storm of protest from Dawley Urban District Council's highways and public works committee whose members felt the work could have been completed a good deal more quickly than was the case.

A new estate of bungalows at 'Wombridge Farm, Oakengates', on a dull February day in 1967. And what happened to Wombridge Farm? It was demolished to make way for the new homes, of course.

Flooding at Dale End, Coalbrookdale, on December 12, 1965. Dale End only gets under water in the severest River Severn floods. The shack-style shop on the right was a familiar sight on the Coalbrookdale scene for many years, before eventually being replaced with a permanent brick structure. In the distance is a single cooling tower for the new Ironbridge power station, on which construction had started a short time previously. Three other cooling towers would quickly join it on the skyline.

Ouch, that hurt! A little MG has come to grief in Southall Road, Dawley, during one of the worst storms in living memory, on July 2, 1968. An hour-long barrage of hailstones bigger than golf balls was followed by severe flash flooding.

There's a definite bounce in the air for these skittish youngsters, enjoying the start of a new season back in 1971. Amanda Newbury, nine, of Stonedale, Sutton Hill; Karen Winter, eight, of Southfields, Sutton Hill; and Yvette Harris-Jones, eight, of Stonedale, Sutton Hill, are jumping for joy.

Perhaps the most memorable, and most lampooned, slogan for the emergent new town was: 'Telford – For People On The Move.' Critics pointed to the regular comings and goings on the new housing estates and said it really was true, this was a population on the move, and as often as not moving out. The little arrow symbol incorporated in the name Telford was not spared the mockery – it was likened to a matchstick man moving out, with all that was missing being a little suitcase. This poster was one of those being used in late 1968 as part of Telford Development Corporation's drive to attract industry and people to the town. A later refinement was the slogan: 'Telford – Your Opportunity.'

Pupils of Phoenix School pick their way through the debris and mud of a construction site within the school grounds. Had Dawley New Town not been superseded by Telford, Phoenix would have become the showpiece school of the new community. The date? – September 1971.

Mrs Jennifer Kilshaw stands outside Ironbridge CofE School on January 13, 1970, after hearing that the school was to be closed down. Mrs Kilshaw, who had an eight-year-old daughter at the school, was one of a number of parents angered by the decision to shut the school and send children to Coalbrookdale CofE School instead. The Ironbridge school had however been having troubles – note the subsidence of the playground. This has happened during half term at the end of May 1969, brought on by heavy rain. The playground sank in places by over 2ft and so children were taught instead at the Coalbrookdale school.

Spring 1971 and traffic makes its way through Trench. Residents complained the road was a 'death trap'. Later on a Trench bypass was built.

Chief executive Mr Andrew Flockhart, nearest camera, heads the chief officers of the Wrekin District Council in April 1974. This was a brand new council, which would take on much of the responsibility for working with Telford Development Corporation to create the new town. It was often a strained relationship, as the corporation was answerable to the Government rather than the elected Wrekin councillors, whose views were often noted – and then ignored. The team – from left – is Mr Godfrey Oldaker (estates director), Mr Simon Barber (secretary to the council), Mr John Davies (finance director), Mr John Linder (technical resources director), Mr John Buckler (planning director), Mr John Matthews (works director), Mr Norman Peel (environmental health director) and Mr Graham Reedman (recreation and amenities).

KNOCK 'EM DOWN

IN 1968 Dawley New Town died and Telford New Town was born, expanding the new town by bringing Wellington and Oakengates within its boundaries. The name Telford came from the great Scottish civil engineer Thomas Telford, who was the first surveyor of public works for Shropshire. At a stroke the size of east Shropshire's new town was doubled.

Telford was going to be a mini city, with an eventual population of around 220,000. Enthusiasm for this great adventure was not easy to find among the local population. And the demolitions which accompanied the onset of Telford did not exactly increase the popularity of the new Telford Development Corporation. To be fair, the 1960s has not gone down in history as a great era for conservation, and many towns across the country were to suffer. Old buildings were knocked down with an almost messianic zeal and those who called for preservation spoke with only a weak voice, which was scarcely heard. In the new Telford, a significant number of buildings lost were slums which would almost certainly have been bulldozed under clearance schemes, new town or not. Many photographs in the following chapters are of Madeley because the redevelopment of that town still rankles with locals to this day. Fine old buildings were destroyed as a traditional street scene was replaced by a shopping precinct, flats, and a library.

A bitter lesson was learnt. Dawley was spared the Madeley experience and, with the arguable exception of Hadley, none of the older towns within Telford was to be treated with such insensitivity again. For Madeley, however, the change of mood came too late.

The Grosvenor Cinema at Oakengates in its final days as a cinema, in the mid-1960s. The film showing is *Those Magnificent Men In Their Flying Machines*. Like so many cinemas in the 1960s and 1970s, it went over to bingo…

...and this was the end of the Grosvenor, on January 13, 1975.

This sad little picture speaks volumes about the story of Telford New Town. The philosophy of 1960s town planning – 'out with the old, in with the new' – could really let rip in an area like Telford. This then is the original Seven Stars Inn, huddling alongside the A5 at Ketley. It was one of the oldest coaching inns on the London to Holyhead road and even boasted that the famous highwayman, Dick Turpin, had once stayed there. The place – although clearly much altered down through the centuries – was said to be the second oldest pub in Shropshire. Built in 1579 as a tavern and posting station, it oozed history. Back in the 16th century, in the days of horses and coaches, the old rutted road ran behind the inn, not in front as was the case when this picture was taken in November 1964. Primitive cobbles and other road surfacing materials were unearthed by men working on the replacement pub. Much of the original wattle and daub Elizabethan building was still to be seen although the walls of the public bar – originally wattle and daub – were by this time covered in plaster. Customers, though, still had to duck their heads under the old Tudor beams and – upstairs – the old bedrooms had sloping floors. Incredibly, the place was demolished only weeks after this picture was taken.

Derelict buildings await the demolition squad at Old Park, near the site of Telford town centre, in March 1973. This area was earmarked for offices and local government buildings.

The pavilion of Madeley Miners Welfare Club in Victoria Road, Madeley, looks the worse for wear in May 1968. It had just been severely vandalised, only two weeks before the club was to disband forever. Windows and doors were smashed or wrenched out, and the club's crockery and four remaining footballs were stolen. Built around 1950, the pavilion was shared with the cricket club and was shared for a time by a youth club. However, it was taken over by Dawley Development Corporation to make way for the Woodside development and a secondary school, and went the way of so many buildings in Madeley during the development of the new town.

Generations of Lilleshall Company workmen and their families had lived and played at The Nabb, Oakengates. But by April 1971 these homes were facing the end, with boarded up windows and grass growing up around their front doors. Oakengates Urban District Council sought a clearance order for numbers 20 to 29 The Nabb. Residents' feelings were mixed. The homes had many memories for them, but on the other hand the properties had unlit outside toilets, no hot water or bathrooms, and were damp and cold.

The Britannia Inn, seen here on May 23, 1974, stood in Castle Street, Hadley, at one of the major entrances to the Hadley Castle works of GKN Sankey. It had been used as the 'local' by Sankey's employees for years. Its bad luck was to be one of 44 pieces of land which Telford Development Corporation wanted to buy compulsorily to build Hadley bypass.

Coalbrookdale War Memorial 'blew its top' in July 1969 – with the aid of a mobile crane. The solid bronze cross, which forms the top of the memorial, was lifted off so that repairs could be made.

It was third pull lucky for the contractors pulling down a pit head at Madeley Wood Colliery in March 1968.

Demolition work in progress on an old property at the corner of Market Street and New Street near the main line railway bridge at Oakengates. The date? January 1975.

The Cuckoo Oak pub at Madeley on February 3, 1970. A few days previously landlord Mr Brian Hill had had an unofficial farewell party as the bulldozers were about to move in to demolish the pub to make way for a new road.

A sad scene inside the Cuckoo Oak shortly before demolition.

A crane swings into action and – as the original caption has it – 'another of Shropshire's hazard spots comes down'. Workmen moved in at Hadley to demolish the Coalport Bridge spanning the main road in April 1967. The bridge had been a hazard for drivers of lorries with high loads. Some had collided with its span. But which was the problem, then? The low bridge or the tall lorries?

Madeley War Memorial gets its marching orders on June 3, 1970. It stood at the junction of Park Street and Church Street and was removed because it was a potential traffic hazard. The new site, agreed with the Royal British Legion, was in Russell Road.

Derelict cottages in Jockey Bank, Ironbridge, on January 29, 1974.

The old railway footbridge at Hadley, photographed in 1971.

Dawley Methodist Church stood at the junction of Chapel Street and High Street and dated from 1860. It is seen here in January 1970, when there was a debate about the merits of the Victorian building. The detractors clearly won, as it was demolished around the late 1970s.

Not everything disappeared forever when Telford town centre was created. Malinslee's Norman Chapel was in the way of the development. It is seen here in April 1971. The chapel was dismantled stone by stone and later rebuilt at Telford Town Park.

'The families moved out nearly a year ago,' reads the 1966 caption to this picture. 'Today, little remains of a group of old cottages in Dawley Bank. Some of the rehoused families who are now living in smart council flats at nearby Powis Place, however, still go back to their old homes. They go back to hang up their washing!' They were not supposed to hang washing outside the new flats so – on a nice day – quite a few of the families went back to use the lines at the cottages.

Madeley Old Folks Rest Room in Park Avenue had opened in 1934, but demolition was imminent in January 1968. A Friday meeting had been held by members every week without a single break, until the last of all on January 12, after which members met in a new building in Church Street provided by Dawley Development Corporation. Opposite the new Rest Room were the old people's flatlets dedicated to the memory of the late R.N. Moore, 'Uncle Bob', who had founded the Rest Room movement after he had seen old people queuing for their pension in the rain on a Friday morning in 1929.

Another one bites the dust. One of the redundant Victorian chimneys at the Lilleshall Company, Oakengates, is toppled on October 28, 1967. The chimneys had taken away the gasses from the boilers supplying the blast furnaces with steam, but they became redundant when the firm changed from coal to electricity. The demolition with gelignite took place at midday that day, a Saturday, and the button on the exploder was pressed by Elizabeth Mason. At the time she and her husband ran a small business doing demolition with explosives, but the insurance cover for this particular job was too much, so it was undertaken by friends from Wolverhampton mostly using their equipment. Elizabeth and the engineer were standing close to the small building in the foreground. 'My husband thought I had been too near, but the chimney was in good condition and we were confident of where it would fall,' she said. 'The tall buildings in the background housed steam engines. They were moved to Blists Hill, but had their piston rods cut in two, which was sad. The other building contained some very interesting vertical steam engines, but they were cut up for scrap, I'm sorry to say.'

The view from Ketley Railway Station onto the platform on February 22, 1968, during demolition. Notice the level crossing gate and old A5 road on the right. The last passenger train through Ketley had been on July 21, 1962.

The Crown Inn in Waterloo Street, Ironbridge, just after Woodside's licensing committee refused to renew its licence on structural grounds in March 1973. Demolition followed.

The Station House at Ketley on the same day as the previous picture. At the time, it appeared to have been saved. Bill Pearson, who had worked on the railways for 43 years and had been tenant in the property – the station master's house – for some years, had bought it only weeks before the demolition gang was due to move in. Bill had fond memories of the platform at Ketley being crammed with people waiting for the 'Ketley Dodger' train and he snapped up the Station House when it was offered for sale. It was only a temporary reprieve for the Station House, as it no longer exists today, and the trackbed of the railway is now a path.

Moor Road in Dawley in September 1963.

The demise of a Telford pub with a grim past. The Queen's Head Inn at Ketley was demolished on September 26, 1973. In September 1950 a beered-up drifter from Bolton called Frank Griffin had popped in to the Queen's Head for a drink. While 74-year-old licensee Mrs Jane Edge had her back turned, he started to help himself from the till. She caught him and confronted him. Griffin struck her and she died. Griffin was convicted of murder and hanged at Shrewsbury Prison in January 1951 in Shropshire's first execution since 1923 – but it was not the last.

One of the chimneys at Randlay Brick Works comes down in May 1971. Two 70-year-old stacks, both 120ft high, were brought to earth to make way for a new road from Brookside, Telford's third housing area, to the new town centre at Malinslee. The company had owned the stacks until two years previously. The plan was to put the rubble from the demolished stacks to good use to form the lower part of an embankment on which the new road, forming the northern boundary of the new Telford Town Park, was to be built. A third stack, about 200ft high and a little older and sturdier than the others, did not suffer the same fate as the other two. It survives as a landmark feature in the town park.

Wombridge Farm estate at Oakengates was under development in January 1967, but this access road winding by the old farm barn was facing closure. The new estate included such streets as Bollingdale Avenue and The Cloisters. Shocked residents at nearly 50 bungalows received a circular letter warning them that they were trespassing by using the access road from Priory Road. At the heart of the problem was a row between the original owners of the site and the developers.

The final stages of the demolition of Wombridge Bridge around the mid-1960s.

People living in 48 prefabs off Moss Road, Wrockwardine Wood, had mixed feelings about a council decision in September 1966 to demolish them. Although their thin walls made them boil in the summer and freeze in the winter, and condensation was causing the metal skeletons to rust, there was a great community spirit. Accommodation was a living room, two bedrooms, a kitchen/bathroom and a toilet. Strangely, Oakengates Urban District Council had undertaken a complete overhaul of all the bungalows, including repairs and repainting, only a month before deciding to knock them down.

The frontage of Bloors shop in Gower Street, St Georges, was described as 'dilapidated and worthless' in November 1972. The building was at least 100 years old and had been empty for years. But the newly-formed Ironbridge Gorge Museum did not share the low opinion of the frontage and rescued the shop by having it dismantled and rebuilt brick-by-brick as a 19th century printing shop at a recreated Victorian town at Blists Hill.

Harry Purcell, aged 84, stands in the street where he had lived for 57 years. It was a shame, he said, that Granville Buildings at St Georges were coming down. Already half the houses were empty, and for the rest it was a matter of time. The photograph was taken on November 18, 1964. They were two-up, two-down homes. One still had gas lighting. They could be rented for well under 10 shillings a week.

The infamous Paradise Lost Club in Hadley in 1972. It was a strip joint which got into hot water for going beyond the bounds of decency, its shows being described as 'lewd and obscene'. It was shut down by magistrates in April of that year and a sensational court case followed. The building itself was demolished.

Children in the playground of Stirchley School in October 1972. The school, which had been built in 1861, closed in December 1972 but every brick was labelled and it was subsequently rebuilt at the Blists Hill Museum. The last headmistress was Mrs Margaret Darlington.

BUILD 'EM UP

ALL the early development of Telford was in the south. In general terms, it has been built from the bottom up. The Tweedale industrial estate was followed by the first really big industrial estate of the new town, at Halesfield. To Sutton Hill goes the honour of being the first housing estate. On March 17, 1967, the Queen came to Sutton Hill to see how things were coming along, and unveiled a plaque. Estates at Woodside and Brookside followed, and these 'big three' had much in common. All were high-density housing estates employing cheap industrialised building process, enclosed within a roughly circular perimeter road. The impression from a distance was of dull uniformity of design. The vast majority of the homes were for rent, the landlord being Telford Development Corporation. Separate garages were provided and were put to all kinds of uses. Some residents even kept their cars in them. On later estates they were expected to keep their motors outside.

In October 1973 the first shops, Carrefour hypermarket and Sainsbury's, opened at 'Telford town centre' – a richly ironic title, as it was in fact in the middle of nowhere. Since then the shopping centre has vastly expanded and there are civic offices, courts, a police station and various entertainments venues. New housing of greater variety has come along, together with a road system incorporating so many traffic islands that visitors get lost very quickly. An attempted remedy has been to create distinctive landmark features on the roundabouts. Despite it all, lingering in the air is an old charge which is still not easily dismissed. Telford is a town without a heart.

Ironbridge Power Station in May 1965. 'With an almost lighthouse appearance, this brick-line reinforced concrete chimney is only a fifth of the size it will be when finished. It will then be 670ft high.' In its finished state it became, and still is, the tallest man-made structure in Shropshire.

Awesome. The Ironbridge B Power Station in 1966. It was called the 'B' power station to distinguish it from the nearby Ironbridge 'A' power station, which had opened in 1932. They operated in tandem for several years but in the early 1980s the 'A' power station was knocked down.

Double take! The giant coolers at Ironbridge Power Station seem suspended over the lower end of Coalbrookdale in this early morning picture from 1972. The low-lying winter sun etches the roadman in the foreground. The power station won a design award and special techniques were adopted in an attempt to make it complement the Ironbridge Gorge. Judge for yourself.

Dawley New Town's first housing development at Sutton Hill in spring 1967. About 20 families had already moved into the 'car-age homes' which had been built during the previous 30 weeks. Second phase of the development, for over 300 homes, was about to get under way in June 1967. Negotiations for the contract had been completed between Dawley Development Corporation and John McLean and Sons Ltd.

Putting the finishing touches to The Red Admiral pub at Sutton Hill on May 31, 1968. Planners built the estate to be self-contained, with its own shops, pub, church – or rather 'pastoral centre' – and community centre.

The Lord Mayor of Birmingham, Alderman Charles V.G. Simpson, unveils the plaque at the community centre at Sutton Hill, in July 1968.

The homes at Sutton Hill were immediately controversial. Critics described them as the slums of the future. Planners went to great pains to keep pedestrians and cars separate, and a maze of footpaths was created throughout the estate. This view is from October 1967.

Hadley's 12-storey block of flats begin reaching for the sky as construction work progresses in January 1967.

Residents of the high-rise Manor Heights flats at Hadley come back down to earth to enjoy the sunshine and fresh air in this picture from the summer of 1972.

The old and the new in Madeley on March 4, 1969. The Anstice Memorial Hall on the right was to survive, but the old shops on the left would not. In the distance is the development of a new Co-op store, with Madeley's new library being created above it.

Rough Farm was finding itself with a lot of new neighbours in August 1970. The houses were the emergence of Telford's second and biggest estate – Woodside. Rough Farm, a Georgian farmhouse, became Rough Park riding stables but fell into dereliction in the 1990s and was severely damaged by fire. It continues to suffer vandalism and arson attacks but, a listed building, has resisted to date the spectre of demolition. Its future must however be considered extremely uncertain.

An aerial view gives a good idea of how Woodside must have looked on the planners' drawing boards. Here the estate is almost complete in spring 1973. The blocks of Woodside houses were given names starting with the letter 'w', such as Woodrows, Waltondale, Wilmere Court... In Sutton Hill they start with 's' and in Brookside, with a 'b'. Woodside's regimented rows of samey homes, couple with confusing numbering, proved a nightmare for postmen. Later Telford Development Corporation tried to break up the uniformity by special painting schemes at Woodside. Residents in the earlier new town estates had the luxury of garage blocks provided for their cars, although in practice they have been used for a wide variety of purposes. On later estates motorists have had to leave their cars in the open.

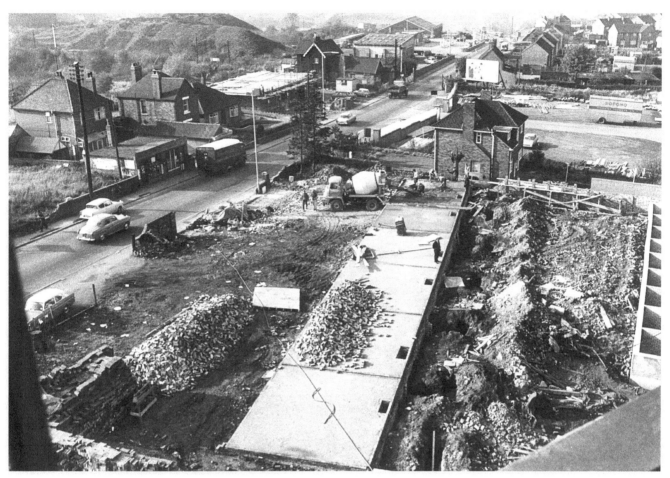

Development continues alongside the A5 at Ketley in October 1964.

Madeley District Centre on October 31, 1969. Not all the shops have yet been let – the boarded up premises became a newsagents and sweet shop. The idea of the centre's design was that shoppers would be able to go about their business in a traffic-free environment. Madeley was the first of the 'traditional' towns which make up Telford to be given such a modern shopping centre, courtesy of Telford Development Corporation. It was also the last. The destruction of the heart of Madeley continues to be much resented by people who remember Madeley as it was and, with the arguable exception of Hadley, no other traditional town in Telford got the same treatment afterwards.

And there's more. The final phase gets going around Anstice Hall in June 1971. Notice that the Co-op, bottom left, has by now opened. Later it was to transfer to the low building, upper centre. It closed in early 2002.

A new Oakengates Telephone Exchange goes up behind the old exchange in May 1970.

That's showbiz! The £126,000 civic hall at Oakengates was growing quickly in this 1967 shot. It was hoped that Miss Jennie Lee, Minister for the Arts, would open it…

…but in the event it was Sir Gordon Richards, one of Britain's greatest jockeys of all time, who opened the completed Oakengates Town Hall in May 1968. Sir Gordon, left, was a local lad, having been born in Donnington Wood, and one of the suites at the hall was named the Pinza Suite after Pinza, the horse on which he won the Derby in 1953. He had left the area nearly 50 years previously. 'When I come home and see all the progress going on, I get lost,' he said, in a commonly-heard remark from people who return to Telford after even only a few years away. When the bills were totted up, the new hall cost £150,000. With Sir Gordon, from left, are Oakengates council chairman Councillor Jabez Davies, clerk Mr B.E. Walters, and Councillor Peter Gibbons.

The new hall was part of a redevelopment at Oakengates town centre. This is the Limes Walk shopping arcade in March 1968.

A new Methodist church goes up at St Georges. The gabled end was approaching 40ft high.

Brookside being built in August 1971.

It's better than telly! Youngsters enjoy the spectacle as a new classroom is delivered to Hartshill Infants School, Oakengates, in January 1970.

A job with a view. Two men worked their way up the outside of the 11-storey Reynolds House, Ketley, in 1967, to repair sealing around the window frames. This was one of the teething problems with the brand new high-rise flats near the A5. With a combination of wind and rain, which is not exactly unusual British weather, water came in through the windows.

A quintessential image of Dawley New Town from November 1967 – houses going up against a backdrop of industry.

Building Telford required the construction of a whole new infrastructure to cope with a population which was, in the early days, predicted to top 200,000. This is work in progress at Coalport's £957,000 sewerage works in July 1969. The site of the works on the south bank of the River Severn was acquired from the Willey Estate, with the exception of a 10ft freeway accessible to fishermen. The works were commissioned the following year to serve over 60,000, but with an ultimate design capacity to serve three times that number.

In February 1973 a party of 'sewer tourists' led by Telford Development Corporation's general manager, Mr Emyr Thomas (right), went down the sewers to see what they were getting for the £10 million spent to date on the sewerage system in south Telford. They saw the surface water sewer which was almost complete which would take rain water from the new town centre at Malinslee, Old Park and Hollinswood. The party entered the 12ft diameter tunnel near the old Stirchley foundries.

A two million gallon water reservoir at Old Park about to be commissioned in June 1970. It was built on high ground so that it could supply the town by gravity. The circular reservoir had an internal diameter of 150ft and cost about £100,000.

Mr John Dugdale, left, chairman of Telford Development Corporation, watched by guests, pours the first skip of concrete to mark the beginning of the first phase of the new Teford Town Centre in March 1972.

This aerial view from June 1974 gives an idea why the name 'Telford Town Centre' seemed distinctly odd – initially there was nothing for a considerable distance around. Essentially the first phase was just a large shopping car park and a couple of major stores. These were the Carrefour hypermarket, and Sainsbury's, both of which opened in October 1973, and are visible beyond the big traffic island. However, new stores were quickly added.

Another picture from the air, taken on July 14, 1974, above the Priorslee Flash pool, which these days has new housing up to the water's edge. It used to be called Hangman's pool or Hangies. The smaller pool on the left was known as the Rough and was a reservoir associated with the Woodhouse pit, which was on the tree-covered area on the left. In between was a pool called The Oily, which lived up to its name. The Lilleshall Company mineral railway to the Woodhouse pit ran along the embankment in the centre.

Hadley has one of the highest proportions of ethnic minorities in Telford. A Sikh temple opened in August 1973.

An exhibition including a scale model of the TV booster station the BBC planned to erect on The Wrekin goes on show at the Shirehall, Shrewsbury, in 1971. One of the first visitors was Cynthia Davies, of Shrewsbury. The Stiperstones were another suggested location for the transmitter, but The Wrekin 'won', in the teeth of opposition from campaigners who thought the mast would ruin the hill. The transmitter became operational in December 1975.

Severn Walk, an area of Sutton Hill, acquired an unsavoury reputation summed up in graffiti on one of the walkways – Welcome To The Bronx. Nobody wanted to live there, and nobody wanted to walk past, which was inconvenient because Severn Walk was on a direct route to the estate's central shops and services. The whole street of homes was empty for many months. In a radical solution, Telford Development Corporation teamed up with McLean In The Inner Cities and redeveloped Severn Walk, turning the 112 flats and maisonettes into 51 private homes in a development renamed Tudor Gardens, which was officially opened by the Earl of Shrewsbury on March 22, 1988.

WELLINGTON'S STORY

FOR those who don't know how the land lies, this is how it is. Wellington is in Telford. Yep, definitely. This can be proven by an examination of a map showing the Telford boundary. Yet to many a proud Wellingtonian, Telford is somewhere up the road. They didn't ask for it, and don't want it. Telford? No thank you. Because Wellington has carved out a niche for itself as an independent state within Telford, it deserves a chapter all of its own. Physically, it has been virtually untouched by the new town development. The Square at the dawn of the 21st century isn't much different to the way it looked at the beginning of the 20th. A robust town council and an active civic society ensure there are influential voices to champion Wellington's interests. The pictures in this chapter prove that the damage done to Wellington in the past has been largely self-inflicted.

There was wholesale demolition in the 1960s, before Wellington was roped in to the new town. The creation of a central ring road radically altered the character of the town, but at least was not as disastrous as the Oakengates ring road which created an internal island there. As long-established names in the centre were killed off by competition, new shops moved in. After over three decades, Wellington has pulled off what seemed impossible. It has developed as if Telford never happened.

The Majestic ballroom in Wellington not long before its demolition. It stood at the top of New Street and had been the venue for regular dances at the so-called Palais de Danse. In its last years it was used as an auction saleroom, and in this view is up for sale. In a previous life the building had served as a school.

Mrs Maureen Round, of Montgomery Road, Wellington, who recalled that some 15 years previously she never missed a Saturday night dance in the hall, takes a seat outside what was the main entrance to the now-demolished Majestic ballroom in February 1976.

The playground at Princes Street Primary School in June 1968. Opened in 1858, the school closed in 1970 and children then went to the newly-opened Ercall Junior School. The old school was turned into the Belfrey Theatre, the home of Wellington Theatre Club, and an arts centre.

It's 1968 and there's plenty of goods on show at Fullwoods army and navy stores.

Note the simple, understated message neatly laid out on the side of the van. Nowadays, there would probably be massive multi-coloured words screaming out from the van, causing distress and 'vision pollution' everywhere it went. The year is 1964 and, only nine weeks after first launching an appeal to provide a van for Wellington WVS Meals on Wheels service, Councillor John Lovatt (centre) is presenting a new vehicle to WVS organiser Eileen Draper (seated at the wheel). Looking on is county WVS organiser Mrs Martin Wilson.

Women of Wrekin Ladies Circle on a theme evening at the Forest Glen in the mid 1960s.

Demolition in Wellington High Street in 1966. The taller building on the right is the Chad Valley toy factory, which was originally a Methodist chapel. It closed in 1980 and later became an antiques centre. After some time lying derelict, it has been undergoing a scheme to turn it into luxury flats.

In July 1961 the first four-storey flats on the High Street redevelopment site were almost ready for occupation. They transformed an area which was once slum clearance property.

Wellington Urban District Council in session in 1956 – believed to be on April 25 that year. 'Stimulated by a genuine desire to secure all possible improvements and amenities for its townspeople, the non-political council of Wellington urban district enjoys a position of high prestige among its West Midland neighbours,' said an accompanying story. It talks of Councillor W.J. Laud, a local bakery and restaurant owner, succeeding Councillor Graham Murphy, head of the Wrekin Brewery Company, as council chairman – we think it's Councillor Murphy in the chair at the start of the meeting. The council chamber was in Walker Street, Wellington, and was reached up a flight of stairs. It is now a restaurant. The other councillors are unidentified, but names to toy with mentioned in the contemporary story are 'father of the council' R.G. Murphy (Graham's brother), Councillor C. Lowe, and council clerk Mr B.H.J. Renshaw.

We're being invited to look at the stables at the Queens Hotel. This picture was taken for a special feature in May 1965 which waxed lyrical about the gable end of cottages next to the hotel where the faded age-worn words 'The Queens and Wrekin Hotels stabling' could still just be made out. The Queens was just one of a number of hotels in Wellington that in the old days had offered stabling. Others were The Cock, the Duke of Wellington, and the Ercall Hotel.

Hiatt College stood in King Street and was a private school which aimed to turn young girls into educated young ladies. The girls with their mauve blazers were a common sight in the town. In its heyday it claimed to be one of the most influential ladies' colleges in the country and the first to provide facilities for the higher education of young women, beating Queen's College in Harley Street, London, by a year. Yet by December 1959 it was all over. The college, which had been struggling for some time, closed its doors for good. Founded in 1847, the college (motto 'Fortis et Fidelis') at one time had up to 160 pupils, both boarders and day girls, but in its final weeks only had 60 to 70 girls. The college buildings were completely demolished after the closure.

The original 15th-century Swan Hotel, probably around the mid-1950s. The roundabout at the junction was replaced by traffic lights in 1958. The hotel was a listed building, but was demolished in 1960 because of death watch beetle. A new Swan Hotel was built at the site.

Haygate Road in about the late 1920s. The shop on the corner was simply called The Stores.

The Duke of Wellington pub in New Street closed in February 1962 or February 1963 and was subsequently demolished. A Fine Fare supermarket was built on the site.

The Belmont Hall, built for the Wellington old people's welfare committee (at a cost of £7,000 in 1961) with funds raised by public subscription. The original caption (from 1964) says 'the hall will have to be demolished when the proposed redevelopment of Wellington is carried out because it stands in the middle of the redevelopment area.' But the hall – officially opened by Lord Bradford – still stands today.

Collapse of a bank. 'A well-known Wellington landmark, Barclays Bank, will be completely demolished by the end of the week,' says the original caption to this picture from November 1961. What was it about town planning in the sixties? Were people allergic to history?

Walking over the Orleton Lane bridge in the middle of the road is not necessarily to be recommended, but you could get away with it back in June 1957.

And look what happened not long afterwards. 'Mothers of children who attend the two local schools in the Orleton Lane, Wellington, area, will be pleased when this new 110ft-long footbridge over the main Paddington railway line comes into use. Children at the moment have to keep to the road over a narrow bridge which has blind approaches.' So reads the caption to this picture from July 1962.

Looking up Market Street on November 8, 1966, towards The Square.

The Christmas lights are up back in December 1967 at The Square. Parking was allowed in The Square then – it has since been made traffic-free.

Compare this with the earlier picture of Wellington Urban District Council. This is Wellington Rural District Council in session on April 26, 1956. The council's offices were at Tan Bank and the council's patch covered a huge swathe of territory in and around Wellington, including Ketley, Donnington and villages to the north. The woman at the left of the high table is Christine Challand (secretary), of Wellington; then comes Albert Phillips (senior assistant clerk) of Donnington; Jack Morris (clerk) from Wellington; council chairman Isaiah Jones, from Lawley; and vice chairman George Hayward from Donnington. Below the chairman, wearing glasses, is housing manager Fred Butterick, while at the other end of the same small table is Harry Wall (surveyor), of Donnington. Councillor William Upton of Ketley is the right hand of the two gentlemen wearing glasses in the first full row of councillors' seats.

Demolition in St John Street in October 1966.

Back in the summer of 1968 10-year-old Pearl Edwards, left, of Stokesay Road, Wellington, felt so sad about famine-hit children she saw on television that she decided to do something about it. She started her own campaign to collect money for Oxfam and was joined by, from second left, school friend Jillian Brown, aged 10, Pearl's sister Lorraine, aged eight, and another school friend Caroline Croft, aged 10. For several weeks they toured the Brooklands estate asking for things like clothes, jewellery and anything people might buy, before holding a sale which brought in £21 16s. Pearl and Lorraine and their friends went on to do more collections, for Cancer Research and for the RSPCA.

Demolition at the corner of Victoria Street and New Street on October 29, 1968. The building had been Frank Sanson's house furnishings shop and had been used in its last years for Army recruitment advertising. It had been bought by the urban council in 1961 and was pulled down because it was considered to be in a dangerous condition. Originally it had been bought to help in the widening of Victoria Street, but, said a newspaper report at the time of the demolition, 'there is no immediate plan to carry out this widening nor is there any intention to provide parking space at this point.' The picture was taken from the entrance to Wellington Methodist Church (itself due for demolition in the autumn of 2002).

Treated like cattle? These bus stands were being described by a councillor as more suitable to the local smithfield than the bus station in December 1968. And when the women standing waiting at the shelters in Victoria Street were asked if they agreed with Councillor T. Brothwood's opinions, they did – saying the shelters failed to keep out the elements.

A 200 ton generator passes the Bucks Head junction on its way from Trafford Park, Manchester, to Ironbridge Power Station in December 1966. Looming in the misty background is Walker Technical College – now Telford College of Arts and Technology.

It's August 1969 and holidaymakers, who travelled by night to avoid traffic jams, create this dazzling display for the camera at the Cock Hotel crossroads, Wellington.

Summer holiday traffic crawls along the A5 between Ketley and Wellington in July 1968. The road was an infamous bottleneck until the M54 Wellington bypass opened on December 11, 1975.

Work progresses in May 1969 on Wellington Urban District
Council's High Street housing development.

A snapshot of life. This most unusual view of Wellington was
captured by a camerman on the top of Constitution Hill with
a telephoto lens. In one extraordinary frame, we have traffic on
Victoria Street, a train at the railway station, a new building
under construction in Church Street, and a gasometer on the
other side of town. The date is June 1970.

Work under way at Christ Church, which had been severely affected by dry rot and woodworm, in December 1970. The rot had infected three quarters of the south wall, and all the south gallery, leading to a repair bill running into thousands of pounds. Workmen had to remove the infected parts. Both brickwork and woodwork were affected.

Schoolchildren enjoy the snow in December 1967.

A snowy scene in the town centre in the mid-1960s, looking up Duke Street.

Constitution Hill School in June 1967. It had been empty for years after closing in 1961. Many Wellingtonians had fond memories of the days when it was a youth club, and for 2d a night provided table tennis, darts, snooker, badminton, netball, cycling, soccer, discussion groups and dancing. In its last days the building had been used temporarily by the junior section of St Patrick's RC School and by the Walker Technical College. It was being prepared for sale by auction at the time of this picture. It was at Constitution Hill School that one famous Wellingtonian started his career. Sir John Bayley, when a young schoolmaster, taught there but left after a disagreement with the governors. He started teaching a few boys in a house in Albert Road – and this grew into Wrekin College.

And this is how things turned out for Constitution Hill School on September 25, 1968. The landmark building standing in a lofty position above the town was demolished, although part of the complex was kept to be used as a Masonic hall.

Demolished shops in New Street were being brought back into use in the spring of 1967. A property developer complained about the continued delay in gaining government approval for a radical reshaping of New Street to create a '20th century town centre'. The aim was to bring the buildings back into temporary use until the decision came through. In the event the Wellington plans were superseded by the designation of Telford New Town in 1968.

The reception room in the outpatients' department at the Wrekin Hospital in 1966.

Members of the 1st Wellington Company's Boys' and Girls' Brigades march to the New Street Methodist Church, Wellington, for a family service in 1968.

Miss I. Braithwaite, matron (left), and Sister V.G. Curtiss sit at the new garden furniture donated in November 1968 to Wrekin Cottage Hospital by relatives, friends and Mrs A. Chamberlin, assistant matron (standing) in memory of her father who died at the hospital.

The Wellington to Dawley road was closed near the Arleston estate for four hours during the night in December 1971 after a lorry shed nine tons of empty bottles. Traffic was diverted and mechanical shovels used to clear the bottles. The bottles carried a request – 'Keep Britain Tidy'.

Wrekin Cottage has been for generations a convenient stopping off place for folk walking up The Wrekin, but has had some low points. In the late 1960s the property was in a vandalised state, with smashed windows and lead stripped from the roof. However it was repaired and reopened as a cafe in 1969. Later it fell once more into disuse, but has since again been revived as a watering hole for walkers.

Partial demolition of the Fox and Hounds pub in March 1973. Although planning permission was given to Wrekin Brewery to knock the premises down and build shops on the site, part of the building was saved and was let in June 1975. The original Fox and Hounds on the site was demolished in 1908.

The historic last meeting of Wellington Rural District Council on March 14, 1974. It was becoming defunct on March 31 under local government re-organisation. Clerk Mr John Inch observed: 'I am quite sure that it will not be the same in the future, and I believe that the friendliness and co-operation is just not going to be present.'

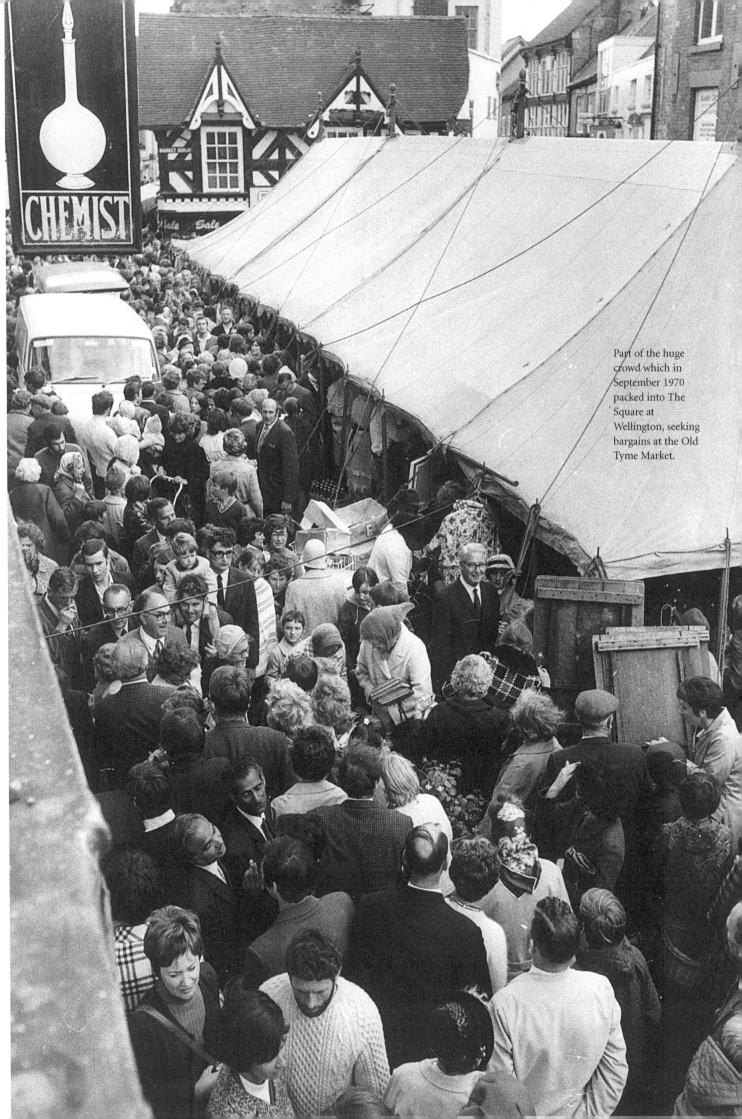

CHEMIST

Part of the huge crowd which in September 1970 packed into The Square at Wellington, seeking bargains at the Old Tyme Market.

Demolition men were at it again – this time in 1974. They were to end the chequered history of what was once King Street Baptist Chapel. After its closure as a chapel it became a soft toy factory and then a radio repair depot.

Wellington's Christmas fairy is seen looking down from the wall of the clerk of the council's office in 1972. And again in close-up!

Fun at Wellington Old Tyme Market in 1975. From left, Ronald Ramshaw, Mark Seabury, David Cobb and William Turner.

Giant piers stand prepared to take the weight of the King Street to Victoria Road section of the new ring road, which was to cross part of Wellington railway station, in January 1974.

Great care was taken in the demolition of a 70ft chimney stack at the former Wrekin Brewery site on January 15, 1975. The operation was insured for £500,000 and 12 one-ounce charges of gelignite were used. Onlookers were moved well back. The demolishers said they needed 105ft of space to bring down the chimney safely, and that they had had just enough. There were rumours that empty beer bottles with messages inside were placed in the chimney when it was built, but nothing was found in the rubble afterwards.

The old Wellington swimming baths in 1981, shortly before demolition. They were opened in 1910 and a stone with that date is now incorporated in a wall a few yards away from the new swimming baths which were built close to the site of the old pool. Wellington swimming club members were given one last free swim at the old baths on November 15, 1981, after which they closed forever.

Chief projectionist at the Clifton Cinema, Mr Nigel Howard, at work in 1979.

It's 1978 and the Clifton is showing Close Encounters of the Third Kind. But what's that to the right of the cinema? Could it be…? The Clifton closed in April 1983 and is now a household fabrics store.

INDUSTRY

HAND in hand with the creation of the homes and infrastructure of Telford went a relentless drive to bring new industries and new jobs. It was in effect a race against time because the traditional industries, foundries, engineering and metal-bashing firms were highly vulnerable in the face of the revolutionary changes which were about to be unleashed. The 1970s were a twilight era. In the following decade much of the old industry in Telford was destroyed, sending unemployment soaring to over 20 per cent for more than six years. Some of the best-known and longest-established firms disappeared forever. Granville Colliery, Shropshire's last coal mine, closed in 1979. Survivors, like Sankey's, saw their workforce dramatically slashed. The 1970s were also the last days of union power. British industry was beset by

strikes, some of which were for seemingly trivial reasons – in 1973 over 300 workers downed tools at Sankey's Hadley plant because the price of a cup of tea in the vending machines had gone up from 2p to 3p.

Our photographs in this chapter capture some of the spirit of the old days, when industrial workers didn't mind getting their hands dirty, firms actually made something, shop stewards wielded almost hypnotic power, and nobody worked behind computer screens. Although it is beyond the scope of this book, in the 1980s a huge influx of inward investment, including the arrival of foreign firms encouraged by the benefits of the newly-declared Telford Enterprise Zone, transformed the situation and sparked off a boom. But my, getting there was painful.

A classic shot capturing the spirit of 1970s industrial relations in Britain. Senior shop steward Algie Fletcher addresses workers at John Maddock & Sons, Oakengates, on August 24, 1972. About 350 workers were in a lockout and pay dispute, and in this mass meeting on the factory car park they voted to reject the management's latest offer. The row was over conditions the management had attached to a pay award ranging from 60p to £1.50.

Sankey's works at Hadley in 1921. Note the canal running behind the works.

A pall of smoke billowed over Hadley on July 26, 1969, when a fire gripped the wheel shop at GKN Sankey. About a quarter of the building was damaged. The fire was thought to have been started by waste material catching light. Four paint dipping plants, electrical equipment and four hydraulic presses were severely damaged. Fortunately the blaze had happened at the start of the fortnight's works holiday, giving time to get things sorted out before production restarted.

One hundred years of mining at Madeley Wood Colliery ends with plenty of smiles in July 1967. The shafts were to be filled and sealed because the colliery could not pay its way. It lost over £220,000 in the year ending March 1966.

Three foremen walked out of the pipe-producting department of Allied Ironfounders Ltd, at Ketley, for the last time in January 1968. After long service at the firm they were retiring early because of ill health. As they clocked out for the last time, about 110 of their mates in the same department were having to give up their jobs after being made redundant. The three foremen, John Parton, 63, of Mannerley Lane, Dawley; Frank Standring, 62, of Windsor Road, Wellington; and Perce Talbot, 61, of Chapel Terrace, Wrockwardine Wood, were presented with pensions benefits.

This is where the cores for the castings were made at the Jackfield factory of Marshall Osborne, this procedure being the first stage in producing moulds for the finished bushes and bearings that the company manufactured. The year? 1969.

Tweedale industrial estate at Madeley, seen here in May 1967, was the first industrial estate of Dawley New Town, with the much larger Halesfield estate quickly following.

The Lilleshall Company's works at Oakengates where spectra glaze bricks were manufactured, photographed in December 1964.

Nearly 500 women workers at the Clifford Williams clothing factories in Dawley and Madeley were embroiled in a dispute in November 1972. It centred over the hiring of temporary workers at the Dawley factory and the dispute there spread to Madeley, where striking women are pictured here on November 10. They are actually standing outside a shop in Hills Lane – the factory itself is in the background over the road. Both the Dawley and Madeley plants of Clifford Williams have since been closed and demolished.

Foreman Bill Dolphin casts an expert eye on the framework foundations of another caravan at the Pilot Works in Oakengates in December 1964.

The times they are a'changin'. The deserted entrance to Blockley's pictured in 1972.

The electric arc furnace used for the production of blackheart iron in action at the Court Works, Madeley, in May 1965. The works closed in 1983 after almost 200 years.

Miners at the Granville Colliery take their lunch break underground in November 1977. From left, Ernest Lowe, John Marlow, Ray Watson and Stewart Braddock. The Granville was Shropshire's last deep mine. It closed in 1979 and uses for the pithead area since have included as a naturist club.

Flying pickets roam through the Brookside estate during the 1972 building workers strike. Pickets descended on sites in both Shrewsbury and Telford. Peaceful persuasion it was not – in Shrewsbury they gathered around a site hut chanting 'kill, kill, kill.'

Recognise anyone? Two pickets chat to police Superintendent Bob Landers (right) during the September 1972 building workers strike. The picket with the beard was Eric Tomlinson – who later became an actor better known as Ricky Tomlinson, star of *The Royle Family* and, in his earlier acting career, the soap *Brookside*. The strike led to a celebrated court case at Shrewsbury Crown Court in which some trade union members were accused of harassment and intimidation.

A general view of the pithead at Granville Colliery in January 1972.

Granville miners take a break in their canteen on March 9, 1965. The young man at the table with his chin on his hand is Malcolm Smith, who later became leader of Wrekin Council and chairman of Telford & Wrekin Council. His smart jacket was bought at Orme's in Oakengates. The miners are watching the draw of names put in a drum. Granville was at this time declared the safest pit in the West Midlands and as a reward the National Coal Board provided a lump sum for distribution among accident-free men with an attendance record of 80 per cent or better. Of 310 names put in a drum at Granville, seven lucky winners received £5 each. Directly under the clock is Alan Mullinder, and next to him with the open necked shirt is 'Cheyenne' Edwards. Next right with a scarf is Arnold Wallace. The man with the beret at the table was called Jimmy, and to the right of Jimmy, looking over his shoulder, is Jack Edwards, brother of 'Cheyenne'. With his face partly hidden by Jimmy's beret and with fair hair is Tony Lucas while at the far top right of the photograph is Ted Jones. The miner standing tall above the others at the end of the serving hatch is Reginald Norton.

The John Maddock foundry at Oakengates pictured in 1965. Workers are illuminated by the glow from the white hot molten iron.

The last day at work for these employees of Maw & Co, the famous Jackfield tilemakers, on January 2, 1970. Over 70 workers lost their jobs when the plant closed.

The yard at Adamson Alliance at Horsehay around the late 1960s. The huge hangar-like buildings at what were known locally as Horsehay Works dominated the landscape.

The interior of Adamson Alliance in 1969.

Enjoying a drink at the Allied Ironfounders Social Club at Coalbrookdale are Mrs S. Whittle and Mrs J. Davies at the Tramps Ball in September 1967.

In November 1966 it was announced that the 164-year-old brickworks at Snedshill was to be closed by owners the Lilleshall Company, hitting the jobs of 85 workers. The plant made sanitary fireclay ware.

Around 700 strikers from GKN Sankey at Hadley met in August 1968 and voted to return to work.

And just for a change, a strike meeting of GKN Sankey's workers… This was in the late 1960s or early 1970s – unfortunately the exact strike is unidentified. In 1970 Sankey's was the scene of one of the most damaging strikes in Shropshire's – and Britain's – history when 5,000 workers were out for six weeks, causing a severe knock-on effect in the motor industry. The strike meetings took place at Sankey's stadium in Hadley, which was in its day one of the finest football stadiums in the county, but later was allowed to become a derelict wasteland.

Queuing for grub in the canteen of Horsehay Works in April 1969…

…and after queuing, it's time to take a seat and eat. When the works closed the firm more or less gave away the canteen building to the local community and it became Horsehay Village Hall.

Industrial relics
at Lightmoor in
February 1971.

The Ever Ready battery factory in Hinkshay Road, Dawley, in August 1977. The plant had a relatively short life. It was built from scratch and started production in August 1956. Most of the workers were women from Dawley and the surrounding area. It closed on February 25, 1994, and it was not long before the building was demolished.

Helen Bates was elected Miss Ever Ready in 1967. Runner up was Kathy Willis, right, and Norma Rigby was third.

Ever Ready batteries are turned out by the thousand at the Dawley factory.

Ever Ready strikers vote to return to work on May 7, 1968. The Dawley workforce had come out in support of a strike at the Wolverhampton plant over the introduction of non-union labour. The location of this meeting was a room in a Dawley pub – probably the factory's 'local', the White Hart, which is nicknamed, for obscure reasons, The Jerry.

A visit in June 1967 by pupils of Newport Modern School to Granville Colliery. They are pictured with the pit's training instructors.

Another hive of industry captured on film – this time in February 1975. Spotwelding in progress at the Automatic Pressings factory at Halesfield.

Sales staff of Arleston Dairies' depots in Wellington, Madeley and Shrewsbury flew from Liverpool Airport for a day's sightseeing in Paris in May 1968. The trip was their reward for winning a sales incentive scheme promoted by their employers, Midland Counties Dairies Ltd.

Graduating and engraving a micrometer drum at precision engineering firm Coventry Gauge and Tool in Madeley in 1968.

Brothers united in industrial action. It's June 1970 and the striking drivers of Glynwed Group are standing at the gates of Sinclair Works at Ketley.

A return to work vote by Telford miners in 1974.

Another vote to return to work in a most unusual strike at Marshall Osborne, Jackfield, on September 1, 1972. The managing director's daughter walked out of her job as a receptionist after having a row with her aunt. Two hundred workers promptly walked out in sympathy.

A church hall and a scout hut were among the places used by more than 100 people at GKN Sankey to get the new piecework prices worked out. The process, which was expected to take about three and a half weeks, involved 150,000 piecework prices.

NEW TOWNSPEOPLE

YOU just can't generalise about 'Telfordians'. They are such a diverse lot. For a start, there are thousands of incomers – this, after all, is what the new town is all about.

Then there is the indigenous population, many of whom are more likely to consider themselves as being from, say, Dawley or Wellington, than from 'Telford'. This is because a lot of different small towns have been joined uneasily into one artificial large town and, to be frank, you can still see the joins. Into this melting pot of humanity we can blend in the significant ethnic minority populations, from the Asians of Wellington to the West Indians in Hadley and those of Serbian,

Hungarian and Polish descent in Trench and Donnington. A new generation is rising of Telford-born, Telford-bred residents, for whom the times before the new town may as well be ancient history.

A shining example is world champion boxer Richie Woodhall, who came to Telford as a tot and was brought up on the Woodside estate. It is a development which promises in future to improve the cohesion and sense of one-town identity in Telford which is somewhat lacking at present. But there are an increasing number of people who like their homes, love the environment, and, like Richie, are proud to say they live in Telford.

Thumbs up from Firemen D. Fellows, B. Peel, E. Woolley (driver) and Leading Fireman A. Whitfield (front), part of the large contingent of Shropshire firemen who left Wellington for fire exercises in London in September 1966. The exercises were held to mark the 300th anniversary of the Great Fire of London.

A ride on the horses and trap at Telford Super Saturday in August 1977. Telford Super Saturday, held annually in the town park, was one of the most successful community events held in the new town, attracting massive crowds in the late 1970s and 1980s. Telford Development Corporation eventually handed over the organisation to the local community. The event continued to run as Telford Show, but without corporation cash and organisational support it gradually petered out.

Helen and Clive Richardson splashing through the puddles at Coalport in February 1973.

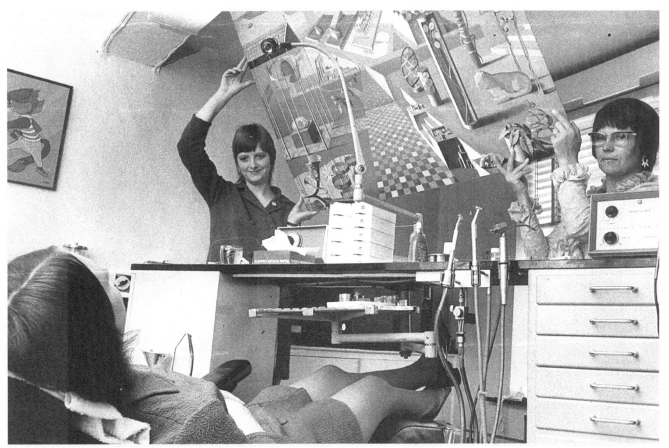

This mural on the ceiling above the dentist's chair in the Madeley dental practice was designed to help patients to relax. Mrs Helen Marrion, of Park Lane, Madeley, was commissioned to paint the mural and is seen fixing it in place, helped by Shirley Smith. Taking the patient's view is dental assistant Jane Pooler. The photograph dates from June 23, 1970.

The Regimental Band and Buglers of the First Battalion, the King's Shropshire Light Infantry, were having a busy fortnight back in May 1965 – 'showing the flag' in their home county and, in this picture, they are seen giving residents of Donnington and the Arleston estate at Wellington a musical treat. The two young lads seen in the picture clearly wanted a closer look.

Wellington RC Junior School is visited by the Lilliput Theatre puppet company in the November of 1965.

A group of fourth-form boys at Trench Boys' Modern School discovered there was rather more to taking a photograph than simply pressing a button. Under the guidance of science master Humphrey Barbier, they made their own pinhole camera.

A Wellington play area at Dothill in April 1968.

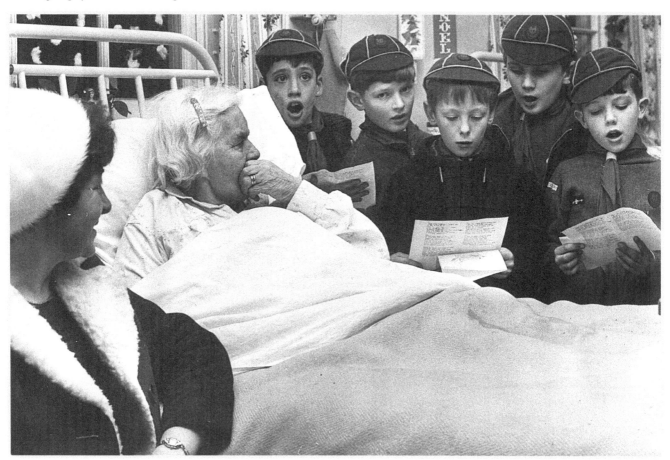

Cubs of the 2nd Wellington troop who visited Wrekin Hospital to sing carols to the patients over Christmas 1967. From left: Cubs Ian Pendlebury, Trevor Brice, David Corbett, Simon Stubbs and Martin Davies, with patient Mrs A. Phaysey of Oakengates, and her daughter, Mrs W. Meredith.

Elderly folk from St Georges Good Companions Club give a cheery wave before setting out for a day trip to Bourton-on-the-Water in the summer of 1967.

Wellington Methodist Youth Centre members set off on a 24-mile walk in aid of Oxfam in the April of 1968.

Showing a little bit of leg, the ladies of Donnington Garrison Amateur Dramatic and Operatic Society were in rehearsal for The Pyjama Game in June 1974. The show was to be presented at the Little Theatre, Donnington. From left: Peggy Evans, Carole Robertson, Marline Vince, Jill Hicks, Lesley O'Neil, Marilyn Lloyd and Kim Cooper.

A fire drill at Wellington fire station on October 25, 1964. Competition drills were being held there at the time and these are not Wellington firemen, but firefighters from Clun – from left, Jack Swain, Ken Lunn, Jim Cook, and Eric Davies.

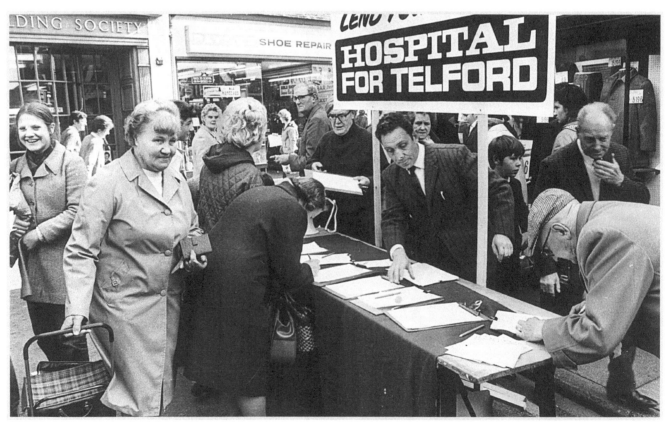

Wellington shoppers sign a petition in The Square calling for the building of a hospital for Telford. The petition was organised by Telford and District Trades Council – in other words, the unions. Thousands of signatures were eventually gathered to be presented to the Government. The proposed site of the hospital was at Nedge Hill, Stirchley. After many twists and turns in the story, it was finally built at Apley Castle in the 1980s.

Fifty Telford youngsters travelled to the Shirehall in Shrewsbury in April 1973 with a petition of 2,100 signatures protesting about the lack of youth facilities in the Sutton Hill, Madeley, and Woodside areas. However the chief education officer John Boyers declined to leave his office to meet them outside. He offered to accept the petition from a few representatives in his office, but the youngsters refused to accept this and left. They had arrived on two hired coaches which they had paid for by organising discos. Their organiser was 15-year-old Mandy Farrar, of Willowfield, Woodside, who is front, holding her jacket.

Mr Alf Shepherd, aged 86, of Heath Hill, receives his Christmas dinner chicken from members of Dawley Circle Club who distributed gifts to sick and elderly residents in Dawley in the December of 1968. Extreme right is club chairman, Councillor Henry Anderson.

Mr and Mrs D. Boyle of the Majestic Ballroom (left) present a wooden seat to residents of Charlton Flats, Wellington. Receiving it is Councillor John Lovatt, chairman of Wellington Urban District Council, watched by Mr D. Draper. Seated (from left): Mrs Elsie Stinton, Mrs Alice Hayward and Mrs Mary Griffiths. It's 1968.

Girls at Madeley Court School model the school fashions in September 1972. New school rules gave them a choice of a trouser suit and flowered blouse, a pinafore dress or a skirt, and they could also wear navy or turquoise sleeveless jackets or a turquoise jersey.

Little Susan Wood, six, serves her friends with ice lollies at Woodside Infants' School, in the summer of 1971. Shropshire County Road Safety Officer Mr A.E. John, is seen with Mr G. Moruzzi (left) of Blewshill Creamery, vice-chairman of the Ice Cream Alliance road safety committee, during instruction on road safety with ice cream vans.

Deckchairs, flasks of coffee and sandwiches kept crowds of people happy as they formed an enormous queue in Telford in the September of 1977. They were not shoppers in the rush for bread, however, but music lovers hoping to get tickets for the only concert to be given in the Midlands by the great guitarist, Andres Segovia. People flocked to Oakengates Town Hall from all over Shropshire, some arriving as early as 6am.

Children get to see the new loos at Wombridge County Primary School in the November of 1974. For the previous 20 years the school had been asking the county council to replace the old lavatories at the far end of the playground, without success.

Members of Hadley Rest Room celebrate the 14th anniversary of the opening of the club in April 1967. The entertainment included excerpts from a concert the elderly people had given earlier in the week.

Micky Fudge scores Telford United's third goal with a penalty in the FA Challenge Trophy replay against Dorchester in February 1972. The third round match was played at the Bucks Head and Telford United won 3-1.

Johnny Ray and Geoff Croft celebrate Telford United's victory in the FA Challenge Trophy at Wembley in 1971. Telford and Macclesfield made history as the first finalists of the new competition in 1970, but Telford lost then 2-0. They came back the following year, winning the competition by beating Hillingdon 3-2 after being 2-0 down.

A Sunday morning session for Salvationists in June 1969 at Oakengates. Often the band would be joined by passers-by.

Under a single lamp and in a garage in Woodside, members of South Telford Youth Action Group meet to plan their next move in January 1974. Once more local youth activist Mandy Farrar (leaning on the table, centre), was their organiser. The youngsters had nowhere to hold their weekly meetings to organise community service work on the new estates, so met in the garage of Councillor Norman Jackson, of Waltondale, Woodside.

Trench Secondary Modern School was officially renamed the John Hunt School by Lord Hunt at a speech evening at the school on July 20, 1973. Lord Hunt, right, unveiled the new name board, watched by chairman of governors, Alderman Charles F. Cordingley. Lord Hunt had been the school's patron since it was opened on January 24, 1955. He was the leader of the team which conquered Everest in 1953.

Lollipop lady Mrs Dorothy Amos in action in December 1968 on the A5 at Ketley. At the time she was appealing to drivers to drive on dipped headlights during the dark mornings. Mrs Amos, known as Dolly Amos, was a well-known local character who worked as a crossing warden at Ketley County Infants School for over 25 years. She also trained youngsters for the cycling proficiency test and campaigned for better road safety. After her death at the age of 71 in December 1991 Ketley Parish Council commissioned a plaque in her honour.

Record crowds attended Coalport China factory's open day in September 1973.

Inspecting an eight-day oak bracket chiming clock with eight bells and Westminster chimes in January 1964 is auctioneer Mr Jack Clayton, and his secretary Miss B. Holt. The clock and many other items from Priorslee Hall were coming under the auctioneer's hammer at a public sale at the hall. Mr Clayton had the unusual distinction during his war service, when he was an officer in the King's Shropshire Light Infantry, of being shot by both sides on the same day. During the Normandy campaign, he was first shot in the arm by the Germans. Then, while he was being evacuated in a truck, the vehicle was shot up by an Allied tank, seriously injuring him in the leg.

The 7th Wellington Brownie pack raised £10 at a coffee evening in aid of a WRVS van appeal at Dothill Parish Hall, Wellington, in March 1972, and pictured here serving the coffee is nine-year-old Tracy Elmore of Sycamore Close, Wellington.

Student teachers at the Oakengates Outpost of Wolverhampton Teachers' College who joined a national protest over education and job cuts by boycotting lectures in June 1976.

Bishop Dionisije – head of the Serbian Orthodox Diocese of the USA and Canada – consecrated the Serbian Orthodox Church, St Nikola's, at Donnington, in the summer of 1968.

Spending a day at Wrockwardine Wood School in May 1977 was Brother Cuthbert, a Franciscan monk. He was there chiefly to give a talk on the Franciscan movement, but here he is having lunch with some of the pupils.

Each day, Mrs Sibley (pictured) or one of three other housewives on Sutton Hill, would – back in 1968 – look after more than 50 toddlers aged two to five in the community centre playground for two hours. They would read stories and play games with the youngsters, giving the mums a little taste of freedom.

Councillor Ted Morris, chairman of the Wellington Urban District Council Road Safety Committee, trying out one of Park Junior School's children's bikes after presenting pupils with Cycling Proficiency Awards at the school in 1973. In the background is Mr Tom Martin, committee secretary, and some of the award winners.

In a photography session are fourth year pupils of the John Hunt School, Trench, back in 1976. They are, from left: David Cornes, Kevin Monaghan, Paul Benting, Teresa Drew, Dale Thompson and their model, Wanda Machnicka.

Taking part in Wellington youth organisation's road safety quiz in November 1971 was a team from Wellington Methodist Youth Club. Last-minute looks at the Highway Code were thought advisable. From left: Jane Phillips, Janet Austin, Linda Bush and John Phillips.

June 1973 and youngsters wake up after the first night of a 50-hour peace fast organised by Youth Action Telford at the Wellington Recreation Ground. Wellington Urban councillors described it as an 'irresponsible' way of raising money for charity, and the organisers were forced to comply with the council's ruling that a doctor should be in attendance.

AND FINALLY...

WE could have given this chapter a grandiose title like Conclusion, Summary, or Epilogue. But really it's just a chance to serve up a further selection of photographs and have a look at where Telford is, and where it's going. Most of the development and infrastructure that is going to happen, has happened. Administratively, it is independent of Shropshire, thanks to the new unitary Telford & Wrekin Council set up in 1998 (which became Telford & Wrekin Borough in 2002). It is served by the M54 motorway (opened 1983) and its own general hospital, the Princess Royal Hospital – although there are proposals to merge it with the Royal Shrewsbury Hospital. The 2002 population of Telford stands at around 130,000, which is a far cry from the original dream, which would have seen it becoming a city of 220,000 or more. The business heart looks futuristic, and Telford shopping centre is expanding yet again. But when night falls, Telford town centre becomes a virtual ghost town, a wasteland of empty car parks. Ambitious plans are on the table to liven it up. As for living in the new town, other Salopians still give you a look of sympathy if you say you live in Telford. They are behind the times. There are even parts of Telford which can fairly be described as exclusive and posh these days. Nature has softened the landscape and there is a 'green network' of open areas. Telford is no longer Shropshire's troublesome child. It's grown up.

Police officer Rosemary Smith – in the politically incorrect wording of this picture's original caption – 'adds glamour to the start of the national crime prevention campaign at Wellington' in the February of 1968.

A 1,100-yard pipe which was to take the surface water of Malinslee, Randlay and Stirchley was being constructed in 1969 by Telford Development Corporation. A sewerage pipe for the same area was being built alongside it.

A BBC outside broadcast crew got stuck while working up The Wrekin on January 13, 1967, and had to be towed clear by a local breakdown van. The television team was on its way to the top to establish a TV link between Wrexham and Manchester for a *Grandstand* boxing programme that afternoon.

The old gate house at Orleton Hall, Wellington, was listed as being of special architectural or historic interest in 1962.

Alan Harper at Hinkshay in 1959 on a James 200cc Captain motorcycle. All the houses in the background were demolished.

Lynn Scott, 19, of Admaston Road, Wellington, and Tina Nicholls of Rushmoor, Allscott, who were pictured in The Square at Wellington in 1976 (obviously), displaying the new T-shirts which were part of the campaign for the Wellington Chamber of Commerce '76 Week.

A misty late December day in Coalbrookdale in 1964 when Wellington Road was closed by problem which hits every few years – flooding.

Two Methodist ministers braved driving rain to mark the 200th anniversary of the crossing of the River Severn at Ironbridge by the founder of the Methodist Church, John Wesley. This picture is from March 1979. Guest minister for the event was the Revd Rupert E. Davies (with glasses) who preached at Broseley before crossing the river to preach at the Methodist church at Madeley Wood. He was taken to the riverbank by horse-drawn carriage and then climbed into the punt with local minister the Rev Tony Kinch. Ironbridge coracle maker Mr Eustace Rogers (with cap) and Mr Philip Barnes controlled the punt which passed under the Iron Bridge during the trip.

Drilling for oil on the Iron Bridge? Not quite. This rig was in action in January 1968 as part of investigations into how best to preserve the historic structure, the world's first major bridge made of iron. Built in 1779, it was threatened because the banks of the River Severn were slowing moving together, squeezing the structure at the rate of a tenth of an inch a year. The drilling was taking out core samples behind the bridge's stone abutments – one solution being considered for reinforcing the bridge was to pour liquid concrete behind the abutments. A major programme of work was undertaken in 1973 and 1974 to stabilise the structure by creating a concrete slab on the floor of the river to stop the squeezing effect.

The centuries-old water mill at Leegomery was bought by Telford Development Corporation in 1973 with the aim of preserving and renovating the historic building. It was also fenced off to stop attacks by vandals.

Work progresses to clear the Charlton Mound, Oakengates, in the 1930s. This picture belonged to local vicar and leading light behind the scheme, the Rev Gordon Cartlidge, whose enigmatic caption was: 'Elizabeth (Norwegian) taking lemonade has a chat with this judge (bench judge).' Work on clearing the massive spoil mound dominating the western approach to Oakengates started in 1933 and continued to 1939, and much of it was done by foreign student volunteers. There is an enduring but ultimately unproven story that one of them, a German, later joined the Luftwaffe and that during the war, when ordered to bomb COD Donnington, he deliberately missed because he didn't want to harm all his old friends from Shropshire.

'The line between Stafford and Shrewsbury has ended at Donnington and the lines taken up, leaving the derelict signal box,' said the original caption to this photograph taken on May 26, 1970. Trains continued to run to the COD Donnington Army depot until around the late 1980s, when that line too closed. There are currently controversial proposals to revive the line between Wellington and Donnington.

Dawley's High Street on the eve of its reopening as a traffic-free precinct in September 1980 following months of work. The opportunity was taken to move the Captain Webb Memorial (in the foreground) to roughly its original position.

The quiet of an afternoon at Madeley was interrupted by the sound of the band of the King's Shropshire Light Infantry marching down High Street in May 1965.

Wellington police officers pictured with their panda cars in March 1968.

In April 1976 the road between Park Road, at Old Park, and Hollinswood was severely buckled. The blame lay with opencast mine workings. The weight of the spoil tip forced the road to rise. The National Coal Board said this was the first time it had happened with opencast working.

St Georges Junior School was at the centre of a storm in the spring of 1970 over the conditions. Jeffrey Hancocks, a councillor on Oakengates Urban District Council, claimed there were rats in the building, water running down walls on to electrical wiring, plaster hanging off walls, Arctic conditions in the winter and thin partitions making teaching difficult. The parent-teacher association meanwhile had been pressing for improvements for two years and chairman Alan Brice agreed with the description of the school as a 'disgusting, despicable hovel.' However, the chairman of the school managers, the Revd W.E. Maiden, countered: 'I've never seen water running down the walls... You'd be very lucky to see a rat.'

And here is what the school was like inside. Well, can you see any rats?

A general view of the River Severn during Ironbridge Regatta in 1965.

Shropshire's firefighters were involved in one of their most unusual and difficult rescue operations for many years on February 9, 1977, when they fought for hours to save the life of one of Britain's top canoeists. Brian Kingthorpe, aged 20, and Keith Morris were training on the River Severn at Ironbridge for an international race at Llangollen when their kayak smashed into a fallen tree. Keith was thrown clear, but Brian, from Wednesfield, was trapped in the stricken canoe by the force of the icy water for six hours. Firefighters shinned along the tree to get to him and eventually brought in a crane to the site of the drama near the Bird In Hand pub and managed to haul him clear. Brian was taken to hospital with hypothermia and cuts to his legs. A Wellington firefighter, Charlie Pearson, was treated for exposure.

The mail will always get through. Postwoman Mrs N. Morris braves the snow at Coalport in December 1967.

Fifteen-year-old Judith Poole, of Barratts Hill, Broseley, (left), and 16-year-old Valerie Henderson, of the Moors Farm, Little Wenlock, model the new Coalbrookdale High School uniform on October 21, 1964. The uniform was a bit controversial. Members of Dawley Chamber of Commerce protested that trade was being taken away from local drapers because the uniforms were supplied direct to the school by a manufacturer.

Mrs G. Rickard's bungalow backed on to the Rock Metal Works at Jackfield, which was the subject of complaints by residents. Residents at The Mount protested chiefly about the smoke, but also added noise to the list. A large fan had kept some awake at night. They said the drone from it was reminiscent of a 'squadron of bombers'. The picture was originally published on August 2, 1968.

The old and the new… Haulage contractor Mr John Joseph Brookes, of Preston Grove, Trench, does another job of work, on November 27, 1967. The bubble car had just been sold by Ray Maslin of Wellington to somebody in the Trench area, who had engaged the traditional services of Mr Brookes to collect the vehicle.

You don't have to be on a river to flood, as Hadley found out in July 1968. Roy Jones and Peter Oranjyk found a canoe was the best way to get about.

This is the sort of thing you remember from your school days. On June 4, 1970, a glider landed safely in the school field at the Abraham Darby School, Madeley. The pilot was Mr David Millett, chief instructor at Worcester Gliding Club, who was taking part in a competition, but simply ran out of lift and had to find somewhere to put down. Youngsters are watching the dismantling of the undamaged glider ready to be trailered away. Conditions must have been tricky that day, because around the same time a glider landed on Lilleshall Cricket Club's ground.

Brownies of the 1st Ketley Pack held a display of work and games at the Church Hall, Red Lake, in 1965. Mrs Williams (Brown Owl) is pictured inducting Julie Ransford (left) and Jacqueline Griffiths into the pack, with Mrs Watkins (Guide Captain) looking on.

Don't go there! Undertaker Mr J.A. Russell descends into a family tomb in the graveyard of the old Red Church at Jackfield in April 1966. The church had been demolished a few years before because of subsidence. A family tomb had been smashed open and coffins damaged and Mr Russell went in to inspect the damage. He speculated afterwards that the culprits had wrongly believed the coffins were lined with lead. The tomb was resealed with ash.

A crowd of about 100 people watched tensely as a twin-engined RAF plane took off from a field near Lawley in August 1967. The plane had earlier made an emergency landing on the field. But happily, with a great roar and in a cloud of dust, the aircraft soared into the air without any trouble and found its way back to its base at RAF Shawbury. Piloting the plane, a Pioneer transport used as a training craft, was the man who brought it down in the emergency, 30-year-old Flight Lieutenant Fred Butcher, of Dawley Road, Wellington, so he must have known the landing area well. His navigator was Flight Lieutenant Ray Felton of Shrewsbury.

Preparations begin in April 1974 for another season of work to secure the future of the Iron Bridge, by building a concrete support between the banks of the River Severn to stop movement which had caused the bridge to rise at its centre.

Prince Charles gets a close look at the bridge during a visit to mark its bicentenary in 1979. Paddling in a coracle on the river below was England's last coracle maker, Eustace Rogers.

The aftermath of a devastating fire which hit Pool Hill Junior School in Dawley during the evening of July 31 and August 1, 1977. Arson was blamed. The handsome Georgian-style building was gutted, although from this picture you have to wonder whether the shell could not have been retained and the school rebuilt. However, the building was totally demolished and the nearby modern Pool Hill Infants School was expanded to accommodate the displaced juniors. The new school which resulted was named the Captain Webb School.

It's May 1965 and voted the most popular boy by his colleagues at the 2nd Oakengates Company Boys Brigade is Corporal Derek Elliot. Here, he proudly shows off his trophy to some of the younger lads.

This mysterious structure on the Madeley Wood side of the River Severn, not far from the Free Bridge at Jackfield, caused a lot of head scratching from people wondering what it was. This picture dates from December 1971. In fact it was a wartime relic – a revolving metal gun turret, erected at this spot, no doubt, to protect the bridge below. It remained a local curiosity until it suddenly disappeared in the dead of night in September 1982. Local historian Ron Miles thinks it was stolen for scrap. Look closely and you will see a lifting eye on the top of the dome, which must have made things easier for the thieves. An identical turret still survives near the railway line at Ironbridge Power Station.

Licensee of The Boat Inn at Jackfield, Mr Reg Jones, and his wife, look out of an upstairs window at the Severn flood water which has marooned their appropriately named pub. It is the January of 1968.

Angry parents stopped traffic on July 21, 1973, in Freeston Avenue, St Georges, near its junction with the A5 at Snedshill. The idea was to prevent heavy lorries and motorists using the estate road as a short cut. Tempers flared as some drivers tried to force a way through, and four policemen had to step in. Notice the Raleigh Chopper bike in the foreground – a must-have item for youngsters in the early 1970s.

Members of Nalgo, the local government officers union, held a chicken barbecue at Orleton Hall, Wellington, in September 1968. Enjoying a dip were, from left, Elaine Allen, Janice Jordan, and Joan Rogers.

The aftermath of a devastating explosion in the morning of January 4, 1971. Number 48 Willows Road, Oakengates, was blown to bits in a gas explosion which also severely damaged the two adjoining homes. The five members of the Nock family inside survived. Ironically, they did not have gas – the leak was from a gas main outside. All three homes were subsequently rebuilt. The rebuilt number 48 initially had storage heaters. But after a while the Nocks decided they were inefficient and had gas central heating put in instead.

George Nock, Bill Tranter, and Clifford Briggs, all of Ketley Bank, were walking down the A5 from the Lilleshall Company on Sunday, May 22, 1966, when they noticed a hole in the parapet, and then saw that a bank had subsided. As they directed traffic to the other side of the road, the parapet collapsed. The landslide closed Shropshire's main traffic artery, the A5, at Oakengates. A railway bridge by the Greyhound crossroads partly collapsed, demolishing part of a parapet and the footpath. The bridge took traffic over the disused Wellington to Coalport railway line and carried gas, water, and sewerage mains.

The switch-on of the revived Wrekin Beacon on April 21, 1965. It had been switched off nearly four months previously after being declared redundant. It was saved by donations from a number of people in the district, including a group of businessmen. It was turned on again at a barbecue and hilly-billy event held by the beacon's preservation trust and attended by about 500. The switching-on ceremony was performed by Sally Pilkington, of Bratton, near Wellington, who had the winning ticket in a draw to pick someone for the honour. The money to keep the beacon flashing must have run out quite quickly, as it was turned off again forever later.

The scene in Madeley Hill, Ironbridge, after an explosion and fire at the Ironbridge Metal Company on May 12, 1950. A small fire broke out at the works, which reclaimed aluminium from foil and was set back from the road. The first firefighters to arrive at the scene played on the flames with water, which turned out to be a fatal mistake. There was an explosion heard miles away which killed the firm's Bavarian-born boss, Ferdinand Frankel, and employee Kate Healey, and left 10 people injured, including seven firemen, some of whom were buried in the rubble. The blast made national headline news and, because of the volatile nature of the aluminium foil, the fire continued to smoulder for weeks.

Flooding in Dale Road, Coalbrookdale, around 1960. Note the Plaza cinema, which was an old malt house, on the right.

The Coalbrookdale Museum of Ironfounding opened in October 1959, marking the beginning of a new era which was forever to change the shape of the Ironbridge Gorge. Lady Bridgeman is seen opening the commemorative gates leading to Abraham Darby's restored historic furnace in the project marking the Coalbrookdale Company's 250th anniversary. She chatted to works manager Mr Fred Williams and other dignitaries. Mr Williams had persuaded his employers to open a building which would record the history and changes in the Coalbrookdale valley, and persuaded them to re-excavate the Coalbrookdale furnace where Abraham Darby had, in 1709, discovered the coke smelting process – which sparked a new Iron Age and made possible the Industrial Revolution. By opening the furnace and a nearby building of artefacts to the general public, the seeds were sown for the creation of Ironbridge Gorge Museum nine years later.

Trench Pool around 1949, showing the gasometer of what was then the Trench Gas Works, with the chimneys of Blockleys Brickworks, and also The Wrekin, in the background.

King Street, Dawley, as seen in a postcard which appears to have been franked in 1921 – although this scene could of course be earlier than that.

Wrekin Labour Party agent Mellor Harrison, left, and the successful Wrekin Parliamentary candidate Ivor O. Thomas, just after the result of the 1951 general election. Who, one wonders, are they ringing? Thomas had captured The Wrekin seat from the Conservatives in the 1945 Labour landslide. Mellor Harrison was a Labour stalwart who gave many years service to the party, and also served on Wrekin District Council.

The Lilywhites – otherwise known as Wellington Town Football Club – around 1920. With the cap in the centre of the middle row is the goalie, a Mr Hedgecox, who always played in his cap. On the far left of the front row is Benny Price or Proctor, who used to play for Blackburn Rovers, and came to Telford when he was suspended. Third from left, back, is Jack Churm, who was involved in running the club. Members of the team around this time were Robinson, Field, Dorricott, Bowen, Deakin, Price, Sambrook, White, and Sheldon or Bond. The team were very successful and won the Birmingham Cup, League Cup, the Shropshire Senior Cup and the Shropshire Charity Cup. Wellington Town became Telford United in 1969.

The goalie makes a save from Colin Jagger during Telford United's 2-0 defeat in the first-ever FA Challenge Trophy final at Wembley in 1970.

An early photograph of Lightmoor railway station which opened on August 12, 1907, and closed on July 23, 1962. Lightmoor brickworks is off the photograph to the left, and the road leading to the upper right is Park Lane, Madeley.

The vision behind the creation of Telford New Town is summed up in this view of the extraordinary Darby House, one of the buildings which epitomises the new wave of architecture for which Telford has become known. Such striking structures set Telford apart from the historic market towns which are its Shropshire neighbours.

Work on the Hollinswood end of the M54 motorway in July 1975. The first short section of motorway, opened in December 1975, was known as the Wellington bypass. There were fears afterwards that the rest of the M54 linking Telford with the M6 might not go ahead, leaving Telford with an isolated stretch of motorway. However, the linkup with the national motorway network came in 1983 with the full completion of the M54.

This artistic feature was a centrepiece of the new Telford shopping centre when the first shops opened in October 1973. It was meant to be a sort of modern version of a fountain. Water continually trickled down the threads. Whatever its merits, it did become a talking point.